A BOY'S LIFE

A Boy's Life

JACK DAVIS

Magabala Books

This is a Magabala Book
LEADING PUBLISHER OF ABORIGINAL AND
TORRES STRAIT ISLANDER STORYTELLERS.
CHANGING THE WORLD, ONE STORY AT A TIME.

First published 1991, reprinted 1993, 2013, 2015, 2019, 2020, 2021, 2023
Magabala Books Aboriginal Corporation
1 Bagot Street, Broome, Western Australia
Website: www.magabala.com Email: sales@magabala.com

Magabala Books is assisted by the Australian Government through Creative Australia, its principal arts investment and advisory body. The State of Western Australia has made an investment in this project through the Department of Local Government, Sport and Cultural Industries.

Magabala Books is an independent Aboriginal and Torres Strait Islander publishing house. We acknowledge the Traditional owners of the Country on which we live and work. We recognise and respect the unbroken connections to traditional lands, waters, and cultures. Through what we publish we honour all our Elders, peoples and stories, past, present and into our collective futures.

Grateful acknowledgment is made for permission to retell in this book a few incidents of childhood, which first appeared in the work *Jack Davis: A lifestory*, by Keith Chesson, published by Dent Australia now Houghton Mifflin Harcourt.

Cover Design Carol Tang Wei
Backcover Photo courtesy Jack Davis
Printed by Griffin Press

NATIONAL LIBRARY OF AUSTRALIA
A catalogue record for this book is available from the National Library of Australia

Department of Local Government, Sport and Cultural Industries
Australian Government
Creative Australia

Other books by Jack Davis

John Pat and Other Poems
Jagardoo, Poems from Aboriginal Australia
The First Born and Other Poems

Plays

No Sugar
Burungin
Honeyspot
Kullark and the Dreamers
Our Town

Foreword

It is a great pleasure for me to write this foreword. I am proud to call Jack a friend. Over the years he has encouraged me in my work with his positive and helpful comments. I first became acquainted with Jack through his poetry, which I continue to enjoy, *The First Born and Other Poems* being one of my favourite books. Then later I got to know Jack through his plays.

A writer, whether conscious of it or not, always reveals at least some of their life through their work. Later, when I was working on my second book, I came to know Jack as a close countryman. I will let him tell about that. What impresses me most about Jack's work is his continual striving to do something new. His recent play, *Our Town,* was terribly ambitious, with 27 changes of scene, and was highly successful in Perth. He is hoping to make his next project a one man show, so once again he will be trying something new.

Jack tells me he has scribbled most of his life, but it wasn't until 1968 that his talent was recognised with the publication of his first poetry volume. Since then he has published two other books of poetry as well as three plays, his life story has been written and he has plans for the publication of two other plays.

A Boy's Life is about the trials and tribulations of his early years. It is written humorously, with several passages that I find very poignant. Even as a boy Jack was a keen observer of human character traits, which stood him in good stead for his future work. I particularly enjoyed Jack's memories of his family and school friends. And I laughed over the stories of the pet show and the water tank. He writes so clearly that his memories evoke forgotten childhood feelings in the reader.

When Jack was a boy his imagination was already so highly developed that his mother was convinced he would grow up to be a writer. Her vision for him has been fulfilled. And her pride in him is still being reflected today by the esteem in which he is held by other writers. Jack Davis is a man to be proud of. Read this book and you will come to know and love the boy who grew to be that man.

Sally Morgan

Dedicated to the memory
of Alice and Bill Davis
our mum and dad

Chapter 1

I was the fourth child of a family which eventually grew to eleven. I wish I could say I was born in the bush and delivered by Aboriginal women in the glow of a campfire. Instead, I was born in King Edward Memorial Hospital in a sanitized labour ward assisted by nurses garbed in the crisp blue and white starched linen of the day. My birth was nothing spectacular. I weighed into and straddled the world without too much labour on the part of my mother in the month of March, 1917. We were a robust family, and were kept healthy with lashings of bush honey and strips of red flannel tied around our necks to ward off colds. Not an Aboriginal custom but one derived from English myth and legend.

In Aboriginal terminology my mother and father were Nor-westers. That is they were born in the north of the State in the Pilbara of Western Australia. Mother remembered dimly that she was taken away from her people at Marble Bar and sent to Broome, where she was given to a white family at the age of seven. The white family consisted of ten children, that in itself a remarkable feat in the isolation of Broome at the turn of the century. Mother was lucky in some respects, when one considers what happened to many part Aboriginal children taken forcibly away from their full blood mothers. The Stretch family, which she became literally a servant to, was kind to her. Though they did not send her to school along with the rest of the children.

At the age of fourteen she went out to what was called service. She became a paid servant to the manager and his wife at the local bank. When the bank manager was transferred to Perth and then Northam, mother went with them and that is where she met my dad. Father was taken away from his tribal mother at an early age and was given to a family called Davis. His real father was a Sikh called Bung Singh. Father's name was Bill and, not liking the name of Billy Bung Singh, he took the name of Davis. He worked as a stockman from the age of eight. He remembers holding his boss' horse outside the Roebourne police station while his boss went to obtain a permit which gave him permission to shoot troublesome blacks on his property. The cost of the permit was one shilling.

Father was reticent about his early life and it was only by occasional snatches of conversation between him and mother was I ever able to glean much. As father lived with, and was reared by whites and as his growing up was in the frontier days of the Pilbara and the Kimberley, I suspect he would have been part of any action to curb blacks in those days. I remember on one occasion hearing him tell of an incident where he was caught in the dark some miles from home. He camped in the dry bed of a river and, heaping his blanket up to look like the shape of a sleeping form and placing his saddle at the head, he took his rifle and slept between a cleft in some rocks. In the morning he found a spear embedded in the saddle.

At 25 years of age he found himself in the south of the State in Northam and it was there that he met my mother and they eventually married. Father was a big man and a willing worker and he found employment in several places in the south. He worked in Northam, Grass Valley, the Dingo flour mills in North Fremantle, Waroona, Lake Clifton and eventually Yarloop, a small dairying and timber mill district some 140 kilometres south of Perth. But it is in Waroona that this story really begins.

Father worked for a year in Waroona. He then obtained a job at Lake Clifton some fifty kilometres west of Waroona where he was employed as an offsider in firing a Cornish boiler which supplied power to pump water from the lime lake. Lime as the finished product was trucked to Perth for industrial purposes. Lake Clifton was a tiny community of some 30 people and the little school had no more than a dozen pupils at one time. It was in this isolated community that I had my first journey with real physical pain. It was customary for mother to make a billy of tea and scones and take them down to the boiler room for father's afternoon tea. It was hot and repetitious work feeding wood into the ever hungry mouth of the boiler's furnace. The afternoon billy of tea and mother's delicious scones were always an appreciated break for father and his fellow woiker. This day as usual, we children were grouped around the kitchen table as mother always baked a few extra scones. She poured the boiling water into the family teapot and turned to the buttering of the scones.

My eldest sister Kathleen placed her mouth over the spout of the teapot and simulated drawing tea out of the spout by drawing in her breath. As most children do I copied her. I sucked hard and I swallowed the scalding hot tea. I screamed in agony. Mother alarmed, opened my mouth and looked at my throat and dismissed my crying as being trivial. But when I reached for the castor oil bottle and drank from it, she realised something serious was wrong. She tore off her apron and ran down to the boiler room to tell father what had happened.

There was no doctor or hospital in our small community and the nearest medical help was in Waroona. There were no motorcars in Lake Clifton. Not even any horse drawn vehicle, only the small Government railway engine. I can only remember the rest through a haze of pain. A mattress was placed on the tender and the little engine began the fifty-kilometre journey to Waroona.

The matron from the hospital was waiting for us at the railway station. I dimly remember being placed in the one railway carriage of the milk train which picked up the daily milk from Bunbury and the small sidings and stations on the way to Perth. But on this run it only stopped for a few minutes at Pinjarra and then sped on its way. On our arrival at the Perth railway station I was carried out in the arms of a burly railway porter to an awaiting car which took mother and I to the Royal Perth Hospital. I was operated on immediately, which meant piercing the blisters which had formed in my throat.

Even to this day I can still smell the nauseating, overpowering odour of chloroform. I awoke to see mother sitting at my bedside, hands clasped in prayer. Mother stayed in Perth for a week, spending all of her time with me. When she was satisfied with my progress, and first stressing upon me the fact that she had other children as well as me, she made a tearful departure, but most of the tears came from me. There were no wonder drugs in those days. It was long before penicillin and other antibiotics and my recovery took nine months. Six months of that period was spent convalescing in Perth. Mother and father had friends in the city and I stayed with them between my periodic visits to the hospital. Mother came up to Perth as often as she could to see me. Mother's friends had a little girl called Peggy who was about my age.

One day we meandered down Thomas Street and found ourselves in West Perth. We were hopelessly lost and tried to cross the railway line near the West Perth railway station. As we attempted to slither down the embankment Peggy tripped and fell. She yelled and grabbed me for support and the two of us fell, rolling head over heels down the embankment. Just as we reached the bottom a train thundered past, missing us by a scant metre. Our mothers, who had been looking for us, peered fearfully down the embankment expecting us to be minced meat. Next day mother went to the hospital and told the doctor that she was taking me home and if it was necessary she would bring me back for a checkup whenever it was needed.

Chapter 2

The following year the job finished at Lake Clifton and the little community moved to Waroona. All the families were transported by train and open railway trucks. Some of the men found work in Waroona. Others went further afield. Father obtained a job managing a small farm for Whittakers Timber Company. The farm nestled in the ranges some ten kilometres east of Waroona. It was picturesque and a pleasant place to live, especially for children. The little stream which meandered its way through the property was a favourite place to play in summer and there was always fresh milk, cream and butter for mother's hungry brood.

The following year on a hot summer's day the circumstances of our family changed again. That day a particularly wicked wind blew with a hot breath from the east. Midday we saw the smoke on the horizon, and within two hours the fire was all around us. Father had a small brumby called Bullet and telling mother to take us children down the creek he raced on horseback to release the pigs from their enclosure. The whole eighteen of them joined us in the comparative safety of the water in the creek.

The ten cows and their calves also found their safety in the water, but the fowls panicked and all perished with the buildings, including the house and all our possessions. That put an end to father's attempts at being a farmer. We found ourselves back in Waroona where father's next job was looking after a team of Clydesdales, massive horses which were used to pull the whims loaded with jarrah logs to the small timber mill located in Waroona.

It was the year 1923 that we moved again. Father had lost his job at Whittakers and was working for Millars Timber Company in Yarloop, twenty kilometres south of Waroona. He only saw his family once a week by coming home on weekends. So one cold early Sunday morning we began that which was destined to be our last journey as a family unit. At four a.m. we were awakened and after a cold breakfast we were all bundled aboard two drays pulled by two Clydesdales. Our transport had been kindly lent to us by Millars. Mother drove one and father the other. Clydesdales are huge workhorses and invariably do not go out of a walk. So we bumped and shook our way along the potholed gravel Perth to Bunbury Highway.

To us children it was an adventure. We would climb down from the drays loaded with all our possessions and run ahead exploring each side of the road for bush tucker such as wild berries and prickly pear fruit. By eleven o'clock that morning we had reached our new home. When poor mother saw the tiny weatherboard and galvanized iron hut which was to be our domicile she was horrified and verbally attacked father. But he was a good self-taught builder and within two months of our arrival he had turned the dwelling into a size large enough to accommodate us comfortably, the timber for additions being supplied free by Millars. We settled quickly into the small town life at Yarloop. Us kids settled in well at school, although it was much larger than the one I had started in at Waroona, having three rooms instead of the one. Mother became a member of the local Methodist Church and local euchre club.

Father joined the football and cricket clubs and was in demand as a trainer. Not only at football but also boxing and cycling. He was an excellent masseur. There was always sporting equipment at our house, cricket bats, footballs and boxing gloves. Father would often don the gloves with us boys and show us how to throw or block a punch. He had a motto which he instilled into us early in life. Never strike a man smaller than yourself. If he is bigger, hit him hard. Another of his axioms was: take a punch and give two in return.

Chapter 3

My brother Tommy was the eldest in the family. He was a happy go lucky type of boy with a ready grin and wit to match. Kathleen, the oldest girl in the family, was the possessor of a beautiful voice. Then there was Harold, a deep thoughtful boy who always seemed to be gazing into space. After me came Teddy, the dreamer of the family. Next of the girls was Ethel Edna, prim and proper, every mother's delight. The next was Dorothy, or Dotty as she was called, the fastest runner in the school. Then there was Barbara, the prettiest of them all, and her claim to family fame is that she could swallow the weekly dose of castor oil without a grimace. Next there was May, forever skinny, who ate like a horse but refused to fatten up. Then there was Frank and baby Judith, the youngest in the family, happy and secure with the knowledge that they had so much love and care around them.

I have purposely left description of myself till last. If you can imagine a tall, big boned, tousle haired brown skinned boy with big hands, big feet and blue eyes you would have a fairly good description of me as a boy.

We were a happy family. It was long before the days of television and even the radio was seldom heard. The long summer evenings meant gathering cow dung to burn in the front and back yards of our house to ward off the mosquitos. Pressure packs were not invented then. Sometimes on weekends father and us older boys would go on hunting trips into the hills. This usually meant a catch of kangaroo, wild duck or wild pig. Bush tucker was important because it helped augment the family larder.

Yarloop is a beautiful little place the rest of the world seemed to have forgotten. The Perth to Bunbury Highway skirted the tiny town and travellers usually sped past, seemingly unaware that they were passing the little town which catered for the second biggest railway workshop in the State. The surrounding country was picturesque, small but affluent dairy farms dotted the flat country west of the town.

West again of the dairy farms was swamp country where father would go duck hunting. Not only did ducks inhabit the swamps, but also a variety of bird life such as crows, bitterns, shags, dab chicks and other species of water fowl. Usually us boys would accompany father. When the parent ducks flew as if they were wounded we knew they had ducklings and we would try to find them, but they always evaded us by hiding in the thick reeds and bullrushes which grew in profusion around and in the swamps.

Chapter 4

I remember my first day at school in Yarloop, we had to walk some two kilometres to and from school along a path through lofty redgum and jarrah trees. There were new wonders nearly every day, a new bird's nest, swooping magpies and bush animal or reptile tracks across the path through the bush. When arriving home from school, there was always fresh milk and scones with lots of golden syrup or fresh honey. On this important day at school I was not to know that I would be knocked down by a large dog, have my first fight, have my ear lugged by an angry motorist and be galloped over by a horse.

That day mother went to visit a sick friend, taking the two younger children with her. She packed an extra lunch for five-year-old me and sent me off to school with my ten-year-old sister Kathleen and my two older brothers Tommy and Harold. The teacher looked sideways at the little Aboriginal boy clutching his sister's hand in the way one looks at a silly pup. She directed Kathleen where to sit her small puppy-like brother. I slid into the hard wooden seat and immediately became restless. The teacher, wise in the ways of children, gave me a picture book with large-lettered words. Midmorning came and I gazed hungrily at the cut lunch on the desk in front of me. Food was food and was meant to be eaten. I did not hesitate, I tore open the package dnd seizing a jam sandwich I ate hungrily.

It was then I felt something prodding me in the back. Looking over my shoulder I saw a freckled faced boy about six years old staring at me. I continued munching. The boy hissed at me, "Gimme a sandwich." I shook my head. I glanced quickly toward the teacher who was head down busily marking papers. Freckles prodded me again, this time harder and with the point of a pencil. Suddenly my voice rang out loud and clear throughout the classroom. "Leave me alone," I said. Freckles sat back in his seat with alarm.

The teacher rose and walked to my desk, and speaking briskly, she said, "What's going on here?" Eyes angry in my jam smeared face I replied heatedly, "He stuck a pencil in my back 'cause I wouldn't give him a sandwich." The teacher, a smile lurking on her face called out to my sister Kathleen, "Come and clean your brother's face. He's got crumbs all over the floor." Kathleen came, straight backed, lips compressed, face scarlet with embarrassment. She wiped my face with her tiny white handkerchief and hissed in my ear, "You wait until lunch, I'm gonna box you across the ear and don't think you gonna get any of my lunch." She gave my face a vicious final wipe and flounced back to her seat.

The lunch-time bell rang at last and the children trooped quietly outside only to explode in heller skeller fashion as they ran to claim the best places to eat their lunches. I sat with my sister who had magnanimously given me a sandwich.

I gazed across the playground and saw Freckles sitting quietly eating. Sitting next to him was a girl about Kathleen's age. It was easy to see they were brother and sister. They were equally freckled in appearance. Egged on by some uncontrollable urge, I got to my feet and headed in the direction of Freckles. I stood in front of him. He was eating a large red apple. I spoke to him softly, hands at my side, "You stuck a pencil in my back." I heard my sister's voice, "Jack come back here." Then I said to Freckles, "Twice." I heard Kathleen's voice again, "Come back here Jack; May take no notice of him." That was when I hit him.

My small brown arm, to which was attached a hard brown fist, hit poor Freckles on the end of his snub nose. He fell back against the play shed wall more in astonishment than pain. But when he saw the dripping blood he howled in fear. I heard my sister Kathleen's angry yell as she lunged towards me. I heard Freckles' sister May scream and I knew I had to vacate that area fast. The boys' toilet - no girl would dare go in there. I sprinted across the play yard and other children began running towards the play shed.

Now nearly every family at school owned a dog and they all seemed to come to school' Sometimes they brought their friends with them and sometimes it looked as if there were more dogs at school than children. I was halfway to my haven, the toilet, when I was struck by a hairy avalanche.

I saw the dog but far too late. The dog saw me but that was late too. The canine missile struck me squarely in the chest and I went down in a heap flat on my back. The dog, having four legs, was first on his feet. He stood almost astride of me by now, a reluctant champion. The dog looked at me and giving me the doggie equivalent of a lopsided grin, licked my face once, then careered off across the play yard. It was my eldest brother Tommy who rescued me from my predicament in the toilet by making me wash my tear stained face and telling me quite solemnly that even heroes cry.

School was over for the day. The school itself was some distance from most of the houses in Yarloop. There were a few dwellings in an area called Scrap Iron Terrace because all the scrap iron from the mill and workshops was dumped there. The town was divided into two sections by name. There was the bottom yard, where the workshops were, and the top yard, where all the timber was milled and stacked. Nearly everybody in the town relied on Millars Timber Company for employment.

The main roads of those days were constructed of gravel, not the gleaming black bitumen of today. The horse and buggy, sulky and carts were still kings of the road, though an occasional automobile would chug through the dusty streets of summer or the mire of winter. The drivers of these vehicles were magnificently dressed in white overalls or long white coats, bedecked with helmets and black goggles, and they bounced along the rutted potholed roads in stiff backed splendour.

My first day at school was certainly eventful, because that day I actually saw an automobile engine for the very first time. The school children walked along the road throwing stones and chasing one another, their shrill laughter and calling could be heard in the autumn air. Suddenly we were attracted by the sight and sound of an automobile. We strung out along the road waving and cheering and the dogs began barking and lunging at the wheels, while the driver looked at them with some trepidation as if he expected them to tear his tyres to shreds. He, the driver, was the usual magnificent sartorial figure. Helmeted, goggled, white coated, straight backed, he waved to the children.

Just before the automobile had arrived upon the scene I had plucked a handful of blackboy rushes from the side of the road, and I cheered and shouted along with the rest of the children. One twelve-year-old boy Stan Smith, cried out, "Look the engine ain't got no cover." There was a chorus of voices. Even the usually sedate older girls joined in with the cry, "Slow down mister, slow down," and the marvel who was driving the car slowed down to an obliging five miles an hour.

The automobile drew level with us and for the first time myself and the others gazed in wonder at the workings of an automobile engine. It hissed, spluttered, wheezed and coughed. There was a huge fan which spun madly. The driver sat there clasping the steering wheel and smiling at his admirers. A sort of suspended trance-like feeling took hold of me. Very much like the feeling when I had bloodied Freckles' nose.

The trance-like feeling was suddenly transformed into action. With one swift movement I flung the double handful of blackboy rushes straight into the whirling fan of the engine. The blackboy rushes immediately became as chaff. The automobile coughed as if in protest, lurched into a pothole, then stopped.

For a second or two there was frozen silence. Even the dogs became quiet. One of them decided to leave a message on one of the front wheels. The driver sat in disbelief. He climbed slowly from his vehicle, bent forward and stared at the now silent engine. Then swiftly he leapt forward, grabbed me by the ear and roared, "What did you do that for?" Sister Kathleen grasped the irate motorist by the arm and cried imploringly, "Oh Mister don't hurt him please, he's only my little brother and I'll get Mum to belt him when he gets home,"

I kept my dilated pupils fastened on the driver. Never in my short life had] seen such a red face. Even redder than sister Kathleen's red party dress. Then I started to think. I knew what I had to do and, with a sudden twist of the head, I wrenched myself away from the automobile driver. I ran, and I ran. I glanced back once, twice, and to my amazement the red-faced driver was laughing, actually laughing at me. I heard my sister Kathleen's voice shrill, "I'll tell Mum on you when I get home you see if I don't." My little brown legs worked like pistons and the wind whistled in my ears. I crossed the first street in a rush and I was halfway across the second when disaster struck again.

I was in the middle of the road before I saw the horse artd rider. Then they were upon me. I didn't pause, at least I think I didn't. I just came to a full stop, crouched in the middle of the road. The horse leapt over me, missing my crouching form by a whisker. Then it swerved and the rider sailed neatly over his mount's head to land in a heap not three yards from my still crouching figure. The fallen rider looked at me in a bemused dazed fashion. I slowly rose to an upright position. The rider was now on his hands and knees. I stared at him and

I thought, "His face is red, redder than even that of the automobile driver's." My voice shook as I spoke, "Did, did, did you fall off your horse?"

Then I forgot them, my sister Kathleen, the horse and rider, the automobile driver, all I thought of was home, and I broke into a run, faster, much faster than I had ever run before and your hero was a hero no longer, just a little five-year-old, impulsive boy running to the safety of his home and the comfort of his mother.

Chapter 5

When I was a child the beginning of summer always seemed to be the best time of the year. The days were growing long and the world seemed to have so much wonder in it. The young birds of spring would be gaining strength to fly in their own world. In the evening the wild ducks would fly over our house looking for a haven for the night in the several ponds which were on the outskirts of the town. There was always the smell of woodsmoke in the air from the forestry controlled fires lit in the hills.

Then there was the swimming hole to the west of the town where the water ran cool and deep. The walk to the creek was through small paddocks of high grass, starting to dry in the summer sun. Here the cicadas chirped incessantly and the trees lining the little creek were full of small birds. Sometimes we would fish for minnows with lines of string and a bent pin. On one occasion Teddy and I cooked some of them on the coals of an open fire. I went home and related this to mother. Her reply was a horrified, "Didn't you clean them first?" Scoffing I replied, "They were clean. How can they get dirty, they're swimmin' around all the time."

There was always something new happening around our household. Like the day mother was singing away to herself. Upon glancing out the kitchen window she saw a long black dugite slithering towards her and under the house.

Mother was not one to lose her aplomb in an emergency. She quickly pulled back the piece of worn lino covering the floor and through the cracks in the floorboards she saw the snake curled up underneath the house. She did not hesitate. Grasping the pot of boiling soup she poured it down through the cracks. Mother never burnt that snake to death, but she made it move. It wriggled from under the house, back the way it had come, so fast mother said that even Phar Lap could not have kept pace with it.

We had fried kangaroo for supper that night.

Chapter 6

Mother and father were both good storytellers and sometimes during the long winter evenings after supper we would gather around the huge open fireplace. One of father's favourite stories was about Karda the racehorse goanna. "Now Karda;" father would say, "was once a young man. He was a very happy man, always laughing and singing, but he had one failing, he was very lazy. He would not go hunting and refused laughingly to fetch wood and water for his wife.

"One day his wife became really angry with him. So she went and got a boomerang;' said father solemnly, "and placed one end of it in the fire until it caught alight. Once again she asked Karda to fetch wood and water, and once again, laughing he refused. Then his angry wife picked up the boomerang and threw it at her lazy husband. He ran and he ran, but wherever he ran the boomerang kept following him.

He turned and jumped upwards, downwards, he turned and he twisted. At last he became tired and the boomerang caught up with him, burnt him on one leg and he fell to the ground and became still. Karda looked at the burn on his leg and it gradually became yellow and that is why," father would conclude, "the Karda has a yellow tail."

Father was a big man, over six feet tall and all us boys were tall for our age. We never wore shoes. Footwear was an expensive item during the depression. Most of the kids went to school barefooted. Besides we could climb and run much faster if we didn't wear shoes.

One of my likes was to run in the rain. I used to love the feel of the wind driven showers on my upturned face, mouth open to catch the delicious drops. Another of my thrills was to watch my father shave. The Gillette safety razor was largely unknown and the open blade razor was still in use. I always suspected the razor would slip or father would make an error and blood would spurt from his cut cheek or chin. Every father knows his son and father certainly knew me. He knew I half expected him to cut himself one day when shaving. So he decided to teach me a lesson, at least that's what he thought. This day, before shaving, he got some red dye and mixed it into a red liquid. He began his morning shave with the dye hidden in the bathroom cabinet. I stood in my usual place watching intently. Mother was out in the yard collecting the morning eggs from our small fowl yard. Father said to me quietly, "Go and ask Mother for a towel, son." I went to the back door, just as mother entered the kitchen with a basket of eggs.

Father knew the stage was set. He quickly reached into the cabinet and liberally splashed one side of his face with the red dye. He gave an unearthly yell and lurched out of the bathroom. Mother and I looked in horror. I breathed heavily and said, "Father you've done it, you cut yourself, I knew you would." But poor mother, she yelled and promptly fainted and fell with the eggs upon the kitchen floor.

Chapter 7

There was a short cut from school through bush to our house in the top yard. Sometimes we would play in the sandpits which had been dug out for sand for ballast. Sometimes we would find a bobtail and turn him over with our bare feet. Daring it to bite us, we would poke it with sticks and it would poke out its blue tongue and hiss, then scuttle away to hide itself under twigs or a piece of bark. It was on one such day that I found my talking tree.

I arrived home to find mother treadling away on the Singer sewing machine. Sister Kathleen was sitting on the floor cutting a pattern from the Ladies Home Journal. Mother paused in her sewing and said to my usual request, "Yes you can have a slice of bread and honey." And she added, "How was school today?" My sister looked up quickly from her task. "Mother," she said, "he was fighting with Teddy Smith today." Mother looked at me, a tiny smile lurking at the corners of her mouth. "Was you?" she asked. "No;"I replied, "he was fighting with me." Kathleen looked at mother sadly and said, "And you know Mary Smith is my best friend." I answered her quickly, "What you really mean is Jimmy Smith is your boyfriend." Kathleen retorted hotly, "He is not and Mother if you don't stop him from saying things like that I am gonna box his ears." Mother admonished us both and said, "Kathy you go and peel six large potatoes for me." Kathleen, pigtails swinging, flounced into the kitchen.

I watched mother tuck and straighten the material on the machine. "What are you making?" I asked. Mother sighed at the inevitable question, "This is a dress for myself and if I don't get it finished by tomorrow I won't be going to the Parent's Meeting at the school tomorrow night." I wiped the breadcrumbs from my mouth with my shirt sleeve. Mother said, "You've got a handkerchief, why don't you use it?" "Aw Mother," I replied, "this is what sleeves are for." Mother answered, "No they're not. Next time use your hanky."

The Singer began to hum again. I watched then spoke, "Mother?" "Yes;' she replied through a mouthful of pins. "Do you know what?" Still concentrating on her sewing, mother replied, "Not unless you tell me." I said, "I heard two trees talking today." Mother choked and just in the nick of time saved herself from swallowing several pins by letting them drop from her mouth to the floor. She bent swiftly to retrieve them, but in reality, to hide her silent, shoulder-shaking mirth. I looked at her suspiciously and said, "You're not laughing at me are you?" Mother, wiping her eyes, answered quickly, "No, I almost swallowed a pin. Anyway tell me about these two talking trees."

"Well," I said, "I took a short cut home from the swimming hole through Martin's paddock and there's these two trees, one was sort of leaning on the other." "Yes," replied mother, "then what?" "Well," I said, "there's one big one and one little one." "Smaller one," corrected mother gently. "Yes," I continued. "The little tree said 'Mummy?' and the big tree said 'What do you waaant?'" Mother looked at me and ruffled my hair and gently replied, "Trees always talk when the wind blows. Now you hurry and collect the eggs for me. Father will be home soon."

Chapter 8

I used to walk through the tall grass which grew in the small fields bordering the creek. Here the clover grew wonderfully high. Sometimes I would leave my friends and wander alone among the clover. Sometimes I would pull up bunches of grass and look for little people like elves and fairies under the carpet of green.

I would sometimes catch a scurrying beetle before it ran to hide and tell myself the little people had been too quick and had changed themselves into insects to escape from me. I would catch the little black and yellow ladybird beetles and hold them aloft on my hand and tell them to flyaway horne because their house was on fire and their children all gone. Then the ladybird beetles would flyaway at my words. Sometimes they refused to leave my outstretched hand and I would tell them they were cruel and stupid and put them back on a blade of grass telling them if they lost their house and their children it would be their own fault.

The luminous fungus, a large mushroom-like growth, always grew in early winter and my second eldest brother Harold and I would find one in the day and go back in the late evening to watch it glow in the dark. Then we would go home and relate what we had seen.

One day, after finding a particularly big luminous fungus, I went home and asked my father at supper time what made the fungus glow in the dark (supper time was always question and answer time at our house). "Well," father said, "the fungus really lives on insects. That's why it glows in the dark. The insects are attracted to it, they fly onto the sticky surface of the fungus and are trapped and eaten." I stared at my father in horror and disbelief. "That means," I said, "that that fungus could even be eating elves and fairies." Father replied diplomatically, "Er I don't think so, they wouldn't go near the fungus." "How would they know?" I asked. "Well;" said father. "They're sort of human aren't they?" "No;" I replied. "They are sort of beings but they aren't human and when they hide they turn into grubs and, and beetles and other things." Father looked at me quizzically and said softly, "How do you know that son?" "I've almost seen a lot of them," I replied. Father patted my shoulder and said, "Well, I think we'll leave it for the moment. Anyway perhaps Mother knows more about little people than I do. You ask her." And he added hastily, "When I'm at work."

That night when our household was almost asleep, father said something to mother. Her reply was a drowsy, "Yes, dear?" "Do you know Jack really believes that some insects are gnomes and fairies?" Mother replied, "Let him be, don't interfere with his childhood fantasies. He'll separate fact from fantasy when he gets older." They lapsed into drowsy silence. Then mother said, "Father?" He replied, "Yes." Mother said, "Do you know what?" Father replied, "No I don't." "Well," mother said, "one day that boy is going to become a writer, you'll see." And for the rest of my boyhood, whenever I saw fungus growing in the bush, I would find a slick and smash it into little pieces.

Chapter 9

Freckles and I had long ago forgotten our first collision at school. Freckles' real name was Lennie but all the kids at school called him either Freck or Freckles. The collective Davis nickname was Davo, especially when applying to me and my brothers. It was late spring when a new boy came to school and When the teacher introduced him to the class as Wenceslaus Nickleby, we stared at this new boy with unbounded curiosity.

Wenceslaus was ten years old, short, fat and dumpy. He also wore highly coloured braces, a tie and a tie pin. His clothes were neat and tidy. The lunch-time break came, Freckles and I sat in the play shed eating and sharing our lunches. We watched the new boy eating alone on the seat opposite us. I prodded Freckles. "Ask him his name;" I said. Freckles called out, "Hey what's your name?" The boy replied, "The teacher told you." Freckles said, "Aw come on tell us, we've forgotten." "Well," replied the new boy rather loftily, "my name is Wenceslaus Nickleby."

"Crikey," I muttered, then I said more loudly, "My name is Jack and this," I jerked my thumb in the direction of Freckles, "is Freckles." Freckles said, "Come over here and sit." Wenceslaus rose to his feet and sat next to us and we munched steadily on. I paused in my eating and said to Freckles, "Looks like we gotta give him a nickname." Freckles looked at our new companion and answered emphatically, "We sure have to." I looked at the new boy somewhat dubiously. "All right," I said, "what are we gonna call you?"

"I already have a name and I'm proud of it," answered Wenceslaus Nickleby primly. "What for?" I asked. "Because," said Wenceslaus, "my great great great uncle was captain of a ship which came out to Australia in 1840." "Big deal," I replied. "Anyway we gotta call you something, something short, you know?" Wenceslaus replied with a mouthful of rainbow cake. "Mother doesn't like nicknames." I whooped and jumped to my feet and said. "That's it, we'll call you Nick for short." I bent forward suspiciously and added. "Your dad ain't got a fish shop somewhere has he?" "And what's that got to do with it?" said Freckles testily. "Because," I replied, "everybody called Nick has a fish shop." "How do you know?" queried Freckles. "Because my dad said so," I replied and added with the cruel streak of children, "What is it to be, Nick or Fatty?" Wenceslaus Nickleby of course settled for Nick.

For the first three weeks Nick's mother brought him to school by horse and sulky and picked him up in the afternoon. The Nickleby family lived in a large house on a farm a half kilometre out of town where Nick's father intended to raise stud cattle. After the three-week period Nick walked to and from school as did most of the other children.

Chapter 10

My brother Harold was two years older than I and was big for his age. He was an athletic type of boy. Felix the cat was a cartoon character at the time, in fact he preceded Mickey Mouse on the screen. Felix was a coal black cat with large eyes. One day at school thirteen-year-old Billy Harris called Harold, "Felix." My brother Harold promptly flattened him. Sometimes some of the other boys would yell out Felix, but they always made sure they had a good margin of distance between Harold and safety. They usually placated his ruffled feelings next day by offering him an apple or an orange.

Harold's love in life was reading. He would often sit up at night reading, when mother and father and the rest of the family was asleep. Now we always had pets at our place such as a dog and a cat, and sometimes a pet magpie, which upon growing up would eventually flyaway to join its kind. We even had pet possums. They too would return to the bush. But we always had a family cat. If by any chance it disappeared we promptly got another.

Now my brother Harold was in some respects a serious type of boy and he disliked being interrupted when indulging in his favourite pastime. I usually had to speak to him five or six times before he answered. Then he would gaze at me in a bemused fashion, his mind full of galloping horses or runaway trains, depending on the contents of the book he was reading.

Mother's method of bringing him back to the world around him was to snatch the book from him and yell, "Harold!" I couldn't very well do that as he was much bigger and older than I was. Also I depended on him a lot for assistance throughout the day. One method he used successfully to make me behave as he saw fit was to refuse to help me make a shanghai or bow and arrow, or to help me with my homework.

On this particular night Harold was reading in the kitchen. Teddy and I were in bed. Our bedroom was next to the kitchen. Directly behind my brother Harold was a window which luckily this night was open. The three of us boys shared a double bed and this bed was directly under the kitchen window. We had at that time a particularly amorous tom cat who was always fighting the other toms over various lady loves. Our tom had a permanently ragged left ear and a drooping left eyelid. Father said he was a sucker for a right hook.

I forgot to mention that my brother Harold was reading a book late that night which gave a graphic description of a ghost who went around the corridors of a castle holding his head under his arm, moaning and crying, "I should have kept calm, I shouldn't have lost my head. I shouldn't have lost my head." I missed the presence of my brother Harold in bed beside me. My young brother Teddy was asleep like everybody else and I kept calling out to Harold, "When are you corning to bed?" But I might as well have asked our old torn cat to give up his lady loves, Strangely enough it was our cat who was responsible for my brother Harold deciding to vacate the kitchen.

Suddenly, and I mean suddenly, the quiet of our peacefully sleeping household was split by the most blood-curdling shriek you could ever imagine. Our torn cat had decided to fight one of his rivals in love, right in our kitchen and right under my brother Harold's chair.

In a microsecond Harold's yell caught up and blended with the screeching of the feline battlers. I told you before, lucky that bedroom window was open because Harold flipped over off his chair and, not bothering to use the bedroom door, dived head first through the window and landed, a quivering mass of terrified boy, tail up in the air right on top of my chest,

Then carne father's voice. "What the dickens is going on there?" My father never ever read Dickens (because he couldn't read nor write) but it was a favourite expression of his, Mother carne into our bedroom and after murmuring a few soothing words to Harold she went back to bed. I told of the incident next morning at breakfast and our old house fairly rocked with laughter. Our torn cat was curled up on the window and to this day I'll swear he looked at me and grinned malevolently. Anyway my brother Harold certainly glared malevolently at the cal.

Chapter 11

Teddy was two years younger than I was and looking back on the family it seems as if his imagination was even more vivid than mine, but I think his imagery was different. Mother rarely sent him on errands because of his absent-mindedness. If mother sent him to buy sugar he would bring back salt.

One of the luxuries which father allowed us was one shilling's worth of comics per week. That shilling would purchase six comics. Friday was comic purchase day and our house would usually have neighbourhood children pay us a visit to have a free read of the comics. One of the favourites was called Comic Cuts, with stories of the sea and about trains. It certainly was Teddy's favourite comic because it contained a story of Cowboys and Indians. One intrepid character was called Cowboy Charlie. He would just go about anywhere in the Wild West and he was always at war with the Indians. Of course Cowboy Charlie was Teddy's hero. There was a sandy cart track alongside the mill railway line which ran past our house. Not only was Cowboy Teddy a deadly shot, he was also a very kind cowboy. Teddy usually shot Indians on his way home from school. Every time he shot one or two he would fashion a cross out of twigs and bury his victims. At one time he had 22 crosses stuck up along the cart track. The sandy track was his battleground.

There he crawled on hands and knees peering ahead into the distance. Sometimes he himself would be knocked flat by an Indian bullet or arrow, but somehow he would miraculously recover and blast the murderous Indians right left and centre.

Another character in Comic Cuts was Little Tommy Tring, he could walk through anything. And as Tommy Tring was made of rubber he could stretch his arms and legs to unbelievable lengths. This attribute of Tommy Tring on this day was almost the demise of Teddy.

One rule loosely applied by mother and father was that all of us kids had to be home by five p.m., that being the time father knocked off from work at the timber yard. At five o'clock the mill whistle would blast through the air. On this near disastrous late afternoon Teddy, accompanied by a boy his own age, Bobby Harris, was meandering his way home from school along the path that cut through the bush. Then they discovered the new nest. The two boys looked up at the sloping jarrah tree and the nest some thirty feet above them. Teddy said, "It must be a wattle bird's nest." "No it ain't," replied Bobby, "could be a mud lark." "Don't be stupid," answered Teddy. "Muddy's use mud to build with." Then they heard the unmistakeable kaark kaark of baby magpies.

"Crikey," said Teddy, "magpies." They both looked around swiftly. Only too well do bush kids know of the angry diving swoop of parent magpies. Bobby said quickly, "Come on let's get out of here." "No," breathed Teddy Davis and Tommy Tring, "I'm gonna climb up and have a look at them. You watch out for the maggies."

Teddy began to climb. Like Tommy Tring he had no fear of heights. When he was about twenty feet from the ground and some five feet from the nest he found he didn't have a foothold. He looked around him and gritted his teeth in determination like Tommy Tring.

The only foothold available was a small hollow about two feet up from his existing foothold. It was somewhat smaller than his foot but Teddy was using Tommy Tring's reasoning. That is, if he leapt upwards to the next available branch he could then place his feet into the small hollow in the tree trunk. Teddy leapt upwards and grasped the next branch. At the same time his foot found the hollow and plunged into it up to his ankle and his eyes were on a level with the three baby magpies in their nest. They started screeching loudly, as if expecting Teddy to feed them. But he had seen them and was satisfied and the Tommy Tring part of him swelled with pride. Not for long though. He decided to descend, but when he tried to remove his foot from the hollow he found he couldn't move it.

The realisation that he was trapped hit him harder than any Indian bullet or arrow. He looked down with rising panic and yelled, "Bobby my foot's stuck." Just then the mill whistle blew, signalling five o'clock. Simultaneously came the rush of wings and the wild call of "Look-out, look-out" from the parent magpies. That was when his friend Bobby deserted him. They attacked Bobby with fury, and with an ungodly yell he ran leaping sideways, upwards, arms flailing and spinning in circles in an attempt to evade the diving parent magpies.

The fledgeling magpies looked at Teddy, their questing little beaks a mere six inches away from his dilated eyes. Then a horrible thought struck him. What if the parent birds returned and pecked out his eyes and gave them to their young for supper? He tried again to move his foot but it was wedged fast. He held on, his mind accepting the fact he was doomed. Then the parent birds returned. The female landed some six feet from Teddy's bare head, while the male bird settled with an angry closing of wings not five feet from him.

It was then that Teddy began to yell and with the yelling poured a torrent of tears of self-pity. Then he heard voices. One was the ever so precious voice of his father, and also his mother. Bobby was there too. Father called out loudly, "Hang on there, we'll get you down in a minute. Just hang on."

The parent birds left the tree with a whoosh of wings. Gaining altitude, they came down in a darting swoop on mother as if it was really "Your young for mine" battle. Mother yelled and grabbed father for protection and he, between laughter and concern said, "Don't worry, just keep your head down. I'll climb up and get him." Father was a big man, just on fifteen stone, but very agile for all his bulk. He began to climb the tree.

He was about twenty feet from the ground when daddy magpie came down fast at father's unprotected head. Daddy magpie's beak snapped like a pair of shears. Father jerked his head forward in an attempt to dodge the clacking beak, bumped his head hard against the tree, lost his balance and with a yell plummeted to earth landing flat on his back at the base of the tree.

At the same time Teddy somehow freed his foot and also with a yell fell and landed on top of father, knocking the remaining wind completely out of him. Poor mother and little Bobby Harris had to almost carry the casualties home. Father was okay for work next day but Teddy missed a couple of days' school with a sprained ankle. Anyway the episode meant the demise of Tommy Tring from Teddy's list of heroes, but he still stuck to Cowboy Charlie.

Chapter 12

Freckles, Nick and I nearly always sat together at the school lunch break. Besides, Nick always had lots of cake for lunch, that being an added incentive for me and Freckles to cultivate his friendship. Conversation amongst children is sometimes direct, sometimes aimless. On this particular day I was relating to my two friends the magpie incident. The conversation turned around who could climb the highest out of the three of us. Nick said, "I'm not allowed to climb trees" "Aw, come off it," replied Freckles, "only girls don't climb." "Yeah," I said, "climbing don't hurt you. All you gotta do is hang on. It's only when you fall you get hurt" Freckles looked at me and the thought was simultaneous - the water tanks.

The little railway station at Yarloop was not far from the school. The tank itself was about seventy feet high and was supported by huge wooden piles. It was a favourite nesting place for swallows and an occasional mudlark Freckles and I often climbed up the iron ladder to look for swallows' nests and the element of danger elevated our adventurous spirits. To us it was a familiar playing area, but one forbidden by parents and the stationmaster.

School was over for the day. The three of us wandered aimlessly down the road. I decided to put the unspoken idea between me and Freckles into action. I said, "Let's go down to the railway tank" I could see Freckles was about to suggest some other activity. Then he caught my furiously winking eye.

We paused at Balla's shop alongside the road to the tank, Nick bought a bottle of lemonade and we walked on, sharing the drink We reached the railway tank and walked around and around the ground level railing. I looked upwards at the tank and said, "I think I'll go for a climb." "Me too," said Freckles. He placed one foot on the bottom rung and began climbing quickly up the seventy-foot ladder with me climbing close behind. We climbed to the top, having a good look for the stationmaster,and then down again.

It was Freckles who asked the question. "Righto," he said, "your turn now Nick" "Not on your life," replied Nick "Aw come on," I said. "Look I'll show you." I sprang up the ladder, climbing nimbly to the top then down again. "Come on," I said to Nick. "Have a turn." "No," replied Nick. "Besides I'm not allowed." "Aw come on," said Freckles. "Your mum and dad won't know. Anyway what are you, a sissy?" I scoffed. "Well," said Freckles, "you must be a girl. First time we seen a boy scared of climbing." Nick shouted, "I am not a girl, it's just that I'm not allowed." Freckles and I chorused, "You're a sissy, you're a sissy."

"I'm not," bellowed Nick. "And to prove it I'll fight both of you, one after another." "Aw come on," I said, "we're not lookin' for a fight. Just climb the ladder and I'll tell you what, you climb up and I'll climb up behind you." "Yeah," said Freckles. "And I'll climb up behind Jack." "Go on," I said, "take your shoes and socks off." Nick looked at the iron ladder reaching into what was to him infinity.

But this was a matter of honour. To Freckles and I it was simply a matter of making our friend climb the ladder and with the perversity of the young we enjoyed his reluctance to climb. I hissed at Nick, "'Fraidy cat, 'fraidy cat." And Freckles joined in with equal venom, "Sissy, sissy, sissy." But Nick was just simply afraid of heights. He believed in terra firma and the more firmer the less terror. His cream puff and apple pie stuffed frame shook with fear. But he also knew his very boyhood standing was at stake. So he made his decision. "All right," he said, "I'll show the both of you." He sat down on the pile supports and quickly took off his shoes and socks. He grasped one of the rungs in front of him and placing one foot on the bottom rung he began to climb.

He was about five feet from the ground when he looked down at me. "You coming?" he asked. "Yeah sure I am," I replied. "Getup a bit higher, there ain't no room for me yet." Nick again started hauling his already quivering frame upwards and placing my hands and feet on the ladder I began to climb behind him. Nick began to slow down. "Don't stop," I called out to him. "Keep mavin', you'll be able to see the swallows' nest soon."

Nick was fifty feet and climbing steadily when I called out to him, "Keep goin', you're nearly there and don't look down." But that is precisely what poor Nick did. He stopped climbing. His knuckles gleamed white with the intensity of his terror. I placed one reassuring hand on Nick's left foot and said. "Go on, keep moving." "I can't," whispered Nick "I can't."

It was then I realized if Nick slipped and fell, he could very well fall on top of me and bring us both crashing groundward. I slapped Nick on one quivering leg and said, "All right I'm gonna start climbing down and you follow me." Nick answered in a terrified whisper, "I can't, I can't move." This brought home to me the full impact of Nick's terror. I looked down at the figure of Freckles below. "He can't move, he's scared stiff, he can't go up or down," I yelled. It was then that poor Nick piddled himself. The liquid flow dripped down on my unprotected head and arms. I bent backwards in an attempt to stop the liquid falling on my head. I yelled at the petrified figure above me, "Stop that, you hear me, stop that, you're making the ladder all wet."

The message must have reached Nick's poor benumbed brain because the liquid flow ceased. I threatened, shouted, cajoled, implored and pleaded, but Nick would not budge, not even an inch. I looked down below at the mouth-open Freckles. "Go and get some help quick." And Freckles ran. I looked at the fat calf of Nick's leg only inches from my face. I reached upwards and punched the calf of his leg but the victim never moved. He never even flinched. Now the Achilles tendon is an involuntary sinew which everybody knows is behind the ankle. When the foot is tense, sharp pressure on the tendon compels the foot to move. I didn't know that, but, I knew the situation was a desperate one and called for desperate measures.

I leaned forward, quickly took Nick's tendon between my teeth and bit slowly and gently. There was no reaction from the owner of the tendon. I bit harder and I felt a slight involuntary movement from the offending foot. This time I really sunk my teeth into Nick's tendon and Nick lifted his foot free of the ladder. I reached up quickly and grabbed Nick's left leg and pulled down on it. "Come on," I yelled at him hoarsely, "keep coming down." Nick managed to make the first rung on the downward journey.

The nearest house was the stationmaster's. Mrs Brown, the stationmaster's wife, was weeding her garden when the panting Freckles reached her and told her what had happened. Well, at least he partly told her.

Mrs Brown was vice-president of the local Parents and Citizens Association and she told it all at the next P and C meeting held at the school the following Thursday evening. Mrs Brown was a big woman and imagined she had the gift of oratory. "Yes," she said to the ladies of the Committee, which included Mrs Nick, I mean Mrs Nickleby, Nick's mum. She said, "I've never seen anything so brave in my life. There was Jack, guiding your poor boy Wenceslaus." (This to Mrs Nickleby) "Guiding your poor boy down that ladder. I declare it must be 150 feet high and he brought poor Wenceslaus down and down one foot at a time until they reached the ground."

Then she added, "A most curious thing happened as they both lay on the ground exhausted, Wenceslaus crawled over to Jack and punched him on the side of the head." Mrs Nickleby replied, "Purely reflex action brought about by the relief of being back on the ground, because normally my boy wouldn't strike anyone."

"And I believe," concluded Mrs Brown, "that the Davis boy should be rewarded for rescuing Wenceslaus, therefore I move he be rewarded a free ice cream a day from Mrs Balla's shop for a week." And that was the conclusion of that. Except the ice creams didn't last a week. Nick, Freckles and I got them and ate them all in one day.

Chapter 13

One of the joys of summer was that there was plenty of fruit growing in Yarloop. A lot of the houses in the town had back yard fruit trees. There were figs, apricots, plums and many other varieties of stone fruit. But one of the best places to obtain fruit was from Mrs Wilson's side fence. There the grapes, black and white, hung down in profusion. Besides, Mrs Wilson, who was partly deaf, turned a blind eye to the boys' stealing the grapes which hung over the fence.

School was over for the day and Freckles and I wandered down the road. It was Freckles who suggested that we go and see if there were any grapes left hanging over Mrs Wilson's fence. "Nah," I said. "They'll be all gone by this." But Freckles thought differently, "It might be worth asking her for some."

We reached Mrs Wilson's house and sneaked up to the side fence looklng for grapes, but they were all picked and suddenly there was Mrs Wilson leaning over the fence itself. I was the first to regain my composure. "Hullo Mrs Wilson, how are you?" I roared. Mrs Wilson replied, "I'm fine thank you Thomas and you don't have to shout, I am not that deaf." Mrs Wilson only knew my eldest brother Tommy's name. So she called all us Davis boys Thomas. Mrs Wilson used to play the piano at the silent picture shows, but with the advent of talkies her talent was no longer needed. Sometimes she could almost make the piano music in the local hall sound better than the talkies. She could make it sound sad with Mary Pickford, happy with Clara Bow and almost cry and laugh with Charlie Chaplin.

Tommy, my eldest brother, used to help the man who ran the weekly picture show. He had a son Peter who was Tommy's age. Tommy always got into the flicks free because he used to help Peter set up the film and projection equipment. Mrs Wilson was in the habit of arriving early at the hall to get a run down and length of the particular weekly show. One night my brother Tommy planked out 'Home Sweet Home' with one finger. Mrs Wilson was enthralled and vowed Tommy had untold talent and offered him free piano lessons. He went along to piano practice for a couple of weeks. Then the other boys of his age group teased him and said fifty-year-old Mrs Wilson was his girlfriend. My brother Tommy belted a couple of them up then gave away the piano lessons.

Mrs Wilson smiled at Freckles and me and said, "How would you two like to earn a large bunch of grapes each?" "Yeah," replied Freckles, "what we gotta do?" "Have to do," corrected Mrs Wilson with a smile. "Well," she said, "there's a hive of bees swarming in my back yard, I have a chaff bag in the back shed and what you have to do is knock the bees off the hive into the bag. Do you think you can do that?"

"Yes," I replied. "I've helped my dad do that lots of times." Which really I had not. If my father wanted to capture a hive I would usually be standing a hundred yards away. Mrs Wilson removed her elbows from the fence. "All right," she said, "come in through the front gate." Freckles and I walked into the yard with some trepidation at having to handle a swarm of bees. But the thought of a large bunch of luscious grapes overrode our caution.

Mrs Wilson gave us the chaff bag and pointed to the bees hanging pendulous, like a huge plum, from the grape vine some three feet from the ground. Then I had a thought and I said to Mrs Wilson, "Can we have the grapes first?" "No," said Mrs Wilson firmly. "You must take the bees away then you can come back for your grapes." And she added hastily, "Wait until I go inside first." With that she hitched up her skirt and scuttled inside the house and firmly closed the door.

Now Mrs Wilson's neighbours were the Martin family. Josh Martin worked with my father in the timber yard and they were good friends. Then there was Dolly Martin and their daughter Agnes. She was fourteen years old, a big-boned tall girl with wispy straight, mousey coloured hair. She was one of the brighter pupils at school. She was also crosseyed and because of that affliction she had to wear corrective glasses.

We heard the latch click on the back gate and looked up to see Agnes Martin walking towards us. Her "Hullo" encompassed both of us. "What are you doing?" she added. I replied, "Well we ain't done nothing yet." "Well," said Agnes, "what are you going to do?" Freckles replied, "See them bees there?" He pointed to the swarm, Agnes looked and the look registered. "Oh," she squeaked, "bees." "Yeah," I said, "bees, and what we gotta do is put them bees in this bag and cart them away somewhere."

Freckles grinned wickedly and said, "You can help us if you like." Agnes squinted hard at the bees, the bag and us two boys. Her agile mind could already see herself telling of her part of this operation at the next nature study lesson at school and more marks for herself. "All right," she said, "what do I have to do?" "No," I said, "she'll only get in the way." "No I won't" answered Agnes. "All you have to do is tell me what I have to do." "Okay," I said against my better judgement, "you and Freckles have to hold the bag open under the bees then I'll shake the hive and when they drop in the bag you gotta close it quick, you understand?" Agnes shook her head so vigorously her glasses almost fell off. "All right," I said, self-appointed master of the operation. "Let's move."

The would-be robbers walked up to the bees clustered somnolent in the afternoon sun. "Now," I said, "what you two have to do is get down and hold the bag like this, and hold the bag wide open." My two helpers, ready and in position, waited expectantly. "You ready?" I called out. "Yep," said Freckles. "Yes," said Agnes. I shook the vine but in that fraction of time a lone bee settled on Agnes' mousey hair.
She gave a small squeaky gasp and removed one hand from the bag to slap at the bee. Consequently the bag, instead of being held more or less open, became almost closed and the bees spilled on top of the bag and over the ground. In those

days the intrepid Mrs Bloomer reigned supreme and one of her products was worn by Agnes. In the seconds that followed, my female would-be assistant fell back on her posterior, her waist-to-knee bloomers in full view.

Freckles jumped to his feet and sprang backwards. My reaction was without forethought or perhaps it was out of sheer disgust at the ineptitude of girls. Bending swiftly and scooping up a double handful of now wide-awake bees, I threw them straight at the bloomers in front of me. Agnes' reaction was immediate. With a shriek she leapt to her feet and clasping her hands between her thighs she ran with a curious sideways crab-like motion towards Mrs Wilson's back door. Mrs Wilson, hearing the shriek, opened the backdoor and Agnes hurled herself at the open doorway, knocking poor little Mrs Wilson over backwards in her rush. Freckles looked at me and said, "I'm gitten out of here." "Me too," I replied, and not bothering to use the gate we scaled the back fence and ran.

Anyway the incident had to have an aftermath. At work Josh Martin called my father aside and told him what had happened. Next day when I got home from school father asked me what had occurred. He admonished me by giving me a clip over the ear but there was a grin on his face when he clipped me one. Freckles wasn't so lucky, his father took the strap to him. But the headmaster, upon receiving a note from Agnes' mother about the incident, gave me and Freckles six cuts with the cane.

Poor Agnes was a week away from school. Mrs Wilson escaped unscathed and we never ever went back for our bunch of grapes. Agnes Martin never ever got around to relating her part in the bee removing incident. Though all the older boys at school wanted her to.

Chapter 14

Father brought home a half-grown ginger cat. It was real cute and sister Kathleen claimed it as her very own. It was given to father by Mr Alf Jones, the local unofficial vet. Unofficial because he wasn't a certified vet. But he knew a lot about animals, such as cows, horses and pigs, even ducks and fowls, and because Yarloop was a dairying district as well as a timber milling area, his knowledge was well utilized. Well Kathleen and Ethel Edna, the next sister to Kathleen in age, spoilt that cat something awful.

Father told mother that Ginger had been cut. Then Mother told sister Kathleen he had been cut, because she was nearly thirteen and old enough to know about these things. Well girls being girls, sister Kathleen told Ethel Edna, who was only seven. And she swore on the family oath of God's Honour not to tell anybody else. Ethel Edna looked at her big sister, excited at the prospect of having a secret, and promised solemnly, "No, no I won't tell anybody, but when he has kittens I want one for my very own." "Don't be silly," said sister Kathleen, pausing as she tied a blue ribbon around Ginger's neck. "He's a boy cat and boy cats don't have kittens. Anyway even if he could he can't." "Why not?" asked Ethel Edna. "Because," said sister Kathleen in a sibilant whisper, "he's been cut." "Oh," said Ethel Edna, "the poor thing."

Ethel Edna was a slim child with enormous brown eyes and brown curly hair and she was always sucking the index finger of the left hand. To her, in all her seven-year-old innocence, a cut was a cut foot or a cut finger and she was satisfied. Well at least until Pet's Day.

Pet's Day was held once a year at the Yarloop school and it was always the day the school broke up for the Easter break. On that day you never saw such a bedlam of sight and sound. The variety of birds and animals would have done credit to any zoo. Well almost. There were cows, calves, piglets, possums, guinea pigs, cats, dogs, birds and goannas. The previous year Alec Dunside, the local doctor's son, pinched a rat from his father's laboratory. They were tame but this one bit short-sighted Mrs Wilmot, the postmaster's wife on the hand. She fainted with fright.

She was a big woman and some of the parents who were present got a fire bucket full of water and washed her face, hands and neck. By the time they had finished with her she was almost saturated. She survived the rat bite but finished up with pneumonia. Alec's father, as punishment, took his shanghai away from him for a whole month. Taking the shanghai really hurt.

The judging of the pets was the most exciting part of the day. The judges were four members of the local P and C, including the local Methodist Minister. Children who brought dogs to school never got very far with these judges because there were so many dogs. There were sheep dogs, cattle dogs, blue heelers, pomeranians, kangaroo dogs and bitzas besides other unheard of breeds. Ducks never got too far because they were messy and besides how can you toilet train a duck? The geese were just as bad and inclined to be cheeky. Mice were too small and possums were nearly always asleep. Guinea pigs did well and, while the piglets were popular, undoubtedly the favourites were cats.

It was the day before Pet's Day. Entry fee for the pets at the show was sixpence and sister Kathleen had dutifully paid in her money a month before. A story had been going around the town that there was the likelihood of Pet's Day being cancelled. It was all because of the mess the ducks and geese made and the cleaners threatened to go to their union about it. But as Pet's Day only happened once a year they grumbled and forgot about it. "Thank God," said Mr Green the Methodist Minister. He didn't use the Lord's name in vain because he really meant it. As he was on the local P and C he would have to help clean up the mess, if the cleaners refused.

The previous year Ellie Potter came to the pet show carefully carrying her pet duck perched on top of her mass of red curly hair. Miss Louden the infant teacher approached Ellie with horror in the passage leading to the judging room and said, "Ellie you musn't carry that bird on your head like that, it might have an accident." "It's all right," said perky Ellie cheerily, "I got a nappy on Marmaduke." And sure enough she had a big red handkerchief tied around her duck for a nappy.

The evening meal was over and mother, father and all us kids were sitting in the large kitchen talking. Our house wasn't large enough to have a living room. It was mother who made the suggestion that Ethel Edna be allowed to carry Ginger into the judging room at the pet show for the analysis of Ginger's good points. Sister Kathleen naturally wanted that honour but mother pointed out that little Ethel Edna with her large eyes and yellow frock, carrying Ginger with a blue ribbon around his neck, would make a very appealing picture. Father agreed and said, "Yes little miss you should look real good but you'll have to keep your fingers out of your mouth." Sister Kathleen reluctantly agreed to let Ethel Edna carry Ginger.

Next morning we all rose earlier than usual. The two girls gave Ginger his final shampoo. That was his tenth for the week. Poor Ginger, he was starting to get a haunted look. Too much water I suppose. By midmorning his coat was glistening. As mother was going to the pet show, she decided that Ginger could ride in the perambulator with baby Frank and two-year-old May. So the entire family, with the exception of father (who had to work), trooped off to school.

Cats are usually highly strung animals and Ginger was no exception and although he had been cut, his nerve ends were becoming somewhat ragged. May kept hitting him with her titly bottle and insisted on shoving baby Frank's dummy in Ginger's mouth. The boys talked mother into taking the short cut to school, which was where Teddy shot his Indians. The pad was heavy sand and us boys had to take turns in pushing the heavy perambulator. At last we reached the school.

Sister Kathleen went along with mother to read the programme of events. There Kathleen read that Ethel Edna's position was tenth on the list. Us boys had run off to find our friends. I found Freckles and Nick at the fruit stall.

I told my two companions of the decision to allow Ethel Edna to carry Ginger to the judges. "Seems a lot of phooey to me," said Nick loftily. "I could have brought a pure-bred Persian calf to school if I had wanted to." "Well why didn't you?" replied Freckles. "Because," answered Nick, "you don't get anything out of it." "You do so," I said, "you get a certificate. Anyway my dad says our cat should win because he was well behaved because he was cut." "What you mean," said Nick, "is that he has been emasculated." "No," I replied, "he has been cut." "Well;' replied Nick testily, "it's the same thing. My dad cuts lots of cattle all the time." Freckles asked, "What do you mean?" Nick looked at us, his two companions, in amazement. "You mean you don't know?" he said. Me and Freckles slowly shook our heads. Nick looked around to see if we were out of earshot of everybody and said, "Well you're a couple of dumb kids all right, so I'll tell you." And he did.

The Reverend Green, Mr Alf Smith the local vet, and Miss Louden the Infants' teacher were the judges. At first the Reverend Green gently tinkled the bell on the long table in front of him. But most of the parents had turned up for the occasion and he had to ring the bell hard to obtain silence. The Reverend was a tall thin man with a forward stoop, deep set eyes, a long nose and buck teeth. Father always said the Reverend reminded him of a vulture. Mother said it was sacreligious to say that of a man of the cloth.

The Reverend at last obtained human silence. "Well," he said, "Pet's Day is with us once again and it is good to see that we have the usual number of people and pets." Picking up a piece of paper from the table in front of him he continued, "This year these are the names of ten children who will bring their pets forward to us, the judges. Each child will answer a few questions about their pets, as to care and grooming etcetera." The ten children with their pets queued up along one wall of the room. Little Ethel Edna was at the end of the queue and the judging began.

Willie Boyle was first with his pet bobtail. He walked up to the judges and plonked it on the table. It opened its mouth and poked out its tongue at Miss Louden who had to be restrained by Mr Alf Smith from climbing onto the Reverend's shoulder. Roddy Howell was next with his pet possum, but it was asleep and just simply refused to wake up. Then there was the usual procession of ducks and geese, a couple of pet magpies and of course dogs and some cats. At last little sister Ethel Edna's turn came; she was the final entrant.

She looked pretty in her yellow dress, her brown curly hair tied with a blue ribbon. She had Ginger draped partly over her shoulder and two of her fingers were stuck in her mouth. "Well little girl," said the Reverend, "what is the name of your cat?" Ethel Edna replied, "Well he ain't all mine he belongs to me and my sister."

Sister Kathleen, sitting next to mother in the audience, beamed with pride in being included as part owner of Ginger. "He's very docile," remarked Miss Louden. "What's his name?" "Ginger;' answered Ethel Edna. Mr Alf Smith stroked Ginger's head and said, "He really is a beautiful animal and so quiet." "Yes," said little Ethel Edna, "he's quiet 'cos you cut him." At the little angel's remark the room became silent. "And," continued Ethel Edna, "that's what my sister

Kathleen reckons." She then placed Ginger on the table and looking at Mr Alf Smith she added, "Mr Smith, where did you cut him?" The Reverend gave a brisk, "Ahem." At least I think he did but it sounded a bit like Amen. Then my voice came from the back of the room. "Yeah," I said, "Mr Smith cut 'em off so he won't go tomcattin' around at night." The silence became frozen.

Mother's face was scarlet, while sister Kathleen's was positively vermilion. She clutched mother's arm and said with a whispered groan, "Oh Mother, let's get out of here." "And," I continued, "that's what they call Imasculating." It was at that point that Tommy leapt across the class room at me and slapped me, and the schoolroom exploded with laughter. Anyway little Ethel Edna got second prize.

Mother told father she would have been awarded first prize if I hadn't spoken up and told everybody about Ginger's operation. Mr Alf Smith told father about it at the pub Saturday night and father had quite a few beers shouted for him just for repeating the incident.

Chapter 15

Although mother couldn't read or write, she was a wonderful cook. The traditional English dishes such as Yorkshire pudding and roast beef, and sometimes wild pig were a delight, and her home-made scones and bread won her many prizes at fetes and the like. Mother never worked off standard scales, but she had her own small and large containers which she marked off to her own scale for measuring ingredients.

She cooked in the old-fashioned wooden fuel stoves of the day. She could judge the heat required to practise her culinary art down to perfection. To scorch a cake or overcook a roast was to her a tragedy and, if by chance that did occur, us kids would vacate the kitchen quick smart. This was before the days of packaged food and mother used to make her own macaroni and her own soap powder, years before they became procurable in shops. Spaghetti was a favourite with our family, especially with kangaroo minced meatballs and mother's home-made tomato sauce.

It was midweek and our cat Ginger had been missing for three days. Teddy and I went over to the timber yard and searched and called for him but all to no avail. I suggested to my brother Tommy that Ginger might have gotten over his cut and was tomcatting around. He threatened to clout me one so I wisely changed the conversation. It was late summer and the night was starting to fall earlier and becoming colder. Mother had decided the evening meal should be the family favourite, spaghetti and kangaroo minced meatballs and mother's home-made tomato sauce.

Tommy and Harold were kicking a football in the back yard. Kathleen was cutting out pictures of film stars and pasting them in her scrapbook. The smaller children were playing cubbies under the passionfruit vine. Baby Frank was lying in his cot made of two kerosene boxes while May was pummelling Gyp the family dog with the titty bottle. Teddy and I were over at Tower's place playing Cowboys and Indians at Freckles' house, where he lived with his mum and dad and his sister May and smaller brothers Billy and Frankie.

Their house was about 400 yards from ours. Four sets of railway lines ran between them. The little timber hauling engines with their brass nameplates on the tender (one was called Captain Stirling and the other Kanowna) would bring the huge jarrah logs down from the hills to the sawmill in the top yard where they would be milled, then hauled to the Yarloop railway station. The milled timber would then be picked up by the huge C class Western Australian Government railway engines and hauled to their destination. Mrs Tower called out over her fence, "You two boys had better be going home, it's just on tea time." After a few more imaginary shots we departed for home. On the third railway line we found Ginger.

Father always tried to keep control over the children at meal times. He had to with ten kids. The seating arrangements were nearly always the same at meal times. Five girls on one side of the table, five boys on the other side, with father at the head and mother at the foot. We all took turns at saying Grace. There were three verses to choose from, one being "We thank the Lord for what we are about to receive." The second one was "We thank thee Lord for this gift of food" and the third one was "We thank thee Lord for filling our tummies and our hearts." Father didn't like the last one. He said it gave him indigestion.

We couldn't afford items such as table cloths. Mother's substitute was clean newspaper; then after a meal, the paper would be rolled up and placed in the stove. That's how mother lost her false teeth. She left them on the table one night and Tommy, whose turn it was to clean up after supper, rolled the paper up and placed it in the fire. Goodbye mother's false teeth.

At this particular meal it was Harold's turn to say Grace. He was a meticulous boy in habit and in speech, very slow and deliberate, and if he made one error in saying Grace he would start all over again. Most of us kids would have our forks loaded with food a scant few inches from our mouths, eyes imploring him to finish. Father usually saved us from the agony of waiting for a conclusion by saying Amen before Harold finished and getting a frown of disapproval from mother for doing so.

When mother placed her huge cooking pot on the table, there would be cries of "Good on yer mother" or "Aw you little bewdy," especially when the dish was spaghetti and kangaroo meatballs, as on this occasion one could see the partiy submerged meatballs in a sea of horne-made tomato sauce. This time of the day was mother's moment, it was what she lived for, the appreciation of her culinary art and knowing that her brood could stuff themselves to the utmost.

Everybody began eating and the huge pot of food began to dwindle. Then father asked of nobody in particular. "Well what happened at school today?" It was then that Teddy said, "Yeah, yeah Father we found Ginger." Sister Kathleen looked up quickly. "Where?" she asked, "and why didn't you bring him horne?" "How could we?" I replied. "He was really cut up this time."

"What do you mean?" said mother. "Because," I replied, "he was cut up by the train." "Oh," said sister Kathleen. "Where?" asked father. "On the third line," I replied. "And his guts it was all along the railway line." "Oh oh," said Kathleen. "Shut up," said Tommy. "And," I continued, "his blood and his guts and his meat is all chopped up like this spaghetti and meatballs and tomato sauce." Father roared, "Shut up." But he roared too late, Mother's skin colouring was usually a light brown, but now her face was a curious mixture of green and brown, and she said in a strangled voice like the croak of an April frog, "Oh, Billy, stop them."

Sister Kathleen's face matched that of mother's. Father looked as if he was going to choke. There was tomato sauce running down his shirt front and there were tears in his eyes and to proliferate matters, just as poor mother started to rise from the table, Frank,tipped his bowl of spaghetti, tomato sauce and kangaroo meatballs into her lap, Us kids were not allowed to swear, not even the mildest epithet. Tommy forgot himself and yelled at me and Teddy, "You two shut your bloody mouths." Sister Kathleen said, "Oh oh," in a faint strangling voice and followed mother with a rush out the kitchen door.

In astonishment I yelled at Tommy, "What's wrong? I only answered Father's question as to what happened today." I glanced over my shoulder towards the door and continued, "And what's wrong with them two?" Father, unable to contain himself any longer, exploded into laughter Spaghetti kangaroo meatballs with homemade tomato sauce was removed from mother's menu for months; at least until the memory of Ginger faded.

Chapter 16

Mr George Wills was a middle-aged stockily built man who owned a piece of land some four miles out of Yarloop. He grew vegetables for a living and he used to provide the town with fresh grown produce. He also grew lemons, oranges and lots of stone fruit. His watermelons were enormous and his rockmelons were luscious and sweet. His means of carting his produce to his customers was a spring cart which was pulled by an old bay horse reputed to be about the same age as Mr George Wills himself. He would arrive in town about midafternoon every Saturday and would drive around his various customers until late in the evening. He was a likeable man, very popular and always gave his customers good value for their money, but his enemies were the big boys of the town and Tommy Davis and Mac Jackson were two of them.

Mac and Tommy were always together and were both the same age. One of their favourite pastimes was to climb up the paperbark trees and try and get a quick glimpse of the girls changing into their bathers. The previous year Mac had fallen out of a tree and broken his arm. It didn't stop him though, or Tommy.

One of Mr George Wills' last deliveries was at the local hospital in the late evening. It was there that the boys would lie in wait for him. They would hear and see the cart creak up the gravel driveway which led to the hospital, with a hurricane lamp tied on the back of the cart swinging side to side casting weird jumping shadows on the fence which bordered the hospital buildings. Mr George Mills was no fool and he knew the hospital was a favourite place for boys to lie in wait for him.

It was a fifty-yard walk from the narrow gate up to the hospital kitchen. All the boys had to do was to wait for Mr George Wills to walk from the gate to the kitchen. One of them would peer through the cracks in the fence at the receding figure with his basket under his arm, then the others would leap up onto the cart, stuff pockets with fruit and then they would flee into the darkness. This night the pattern was the same. The week before, Tommy and Mac had seen a picture of Jackie Coogan, who had stolen some fruit from a fruit barrow for some hungry little waifs, and this added flavour to this particular episode.

Mr George Wills was a reasonable man and he talked to quite a few of the boys around town about stealing his fruit. But the raids went on. He had then threatened to carry a shotgun loaded with saltpetre, poison his fruit and horse whip any of the boys he caught raiding his cart. All to no avail. On this dark night it was Tommy who was to leap up on the cart and Mac had to keep watch. Mr George Wills always untied the hurricane lamp and placed it in the cart so he could see his goods more easily in the dark. This night he followed his usual practice. With his loaded basket he walked through the gate and up to the hospital kitchen.

The two boys were crouched in some bushes a convenient distance away. "Now," hissed Mac. The two sprinted to their places, Mac to glue his eyes to the crack in the fence while Tommy leapt up into the cart. He grabbed some lemons, and put them back in disgust. He moved forward in the cart to look for the apple bag. It was then he got caught in the rabbit trap. Just as well that trap had a weak spring. With a gasp Tommy fell backwards out of the cart and in doing so knocked the hurricane lamp over. There was a gush of flame as the hessian fruit bags, partly saturated with kerosene, caught alight.

Now Mr George Wills' horse always slept at that time of night, in fact he was that kind of horse which could sleep even when pulling the cart. But now his was a rude awakening and when he saw the flames behind him and a figure writhing on the ground, he passed wind with such sound and velocity that poor Tommy thought Mr George Wills had fired the promised shotgun at him. As I said, just as well that rabbit trap had a weak spring. Tommy wrenched the trap from his foot and, with Mac breathing down his neck, ran madly away into the darkness.

In seconds Mr George Wills and the night sister were back at the cart. Mr George Wills ran around and quietened the horse. He then climbed into the cart and obliterated the flames. Actually no damage was really done. As I said, Tommy and Mac ran and they never stopped running until they were safely 400 yards away in the bush. Tommy collapsed holding his foot. Mac subsided out of breath beside him. They looked at Tommy's foot. There were only two small scratches. "What did you yell for?" gasped Mac. "You ain't even bleeding." "I don't have to bleed," answered Tommy hoarsely, "and I tell you this much, I ain't gonna raid his mouldy old cart again." "And I'm not either," breathed Mac heavily, and neither of them ever did.

Chapter 17

I was a normal type of boy and had my likes and dislikes for some incidents encompassed by my twelve years of existence, One of the things I was conscious of was my mother's own personal washing being hung out to dry. Father's washing had the opposite effect. His dungarees, flannels or singlets had an air of solid masculinity about them which brought strange feelings and memories of the whiff of pipe tobacco, the ring of an axe biting into a honey tree and the sharp rolling echo of a .303 rifle being fired on a cold misty morning in the hills, or the acrid aroma of woodsmoke emanating from a bushfire.

My feelings had an almost opposite reaction to the sight of mother's personal clothing hanging on the washing line, I disliked it when mother's nightgown or underwear billowed out in the wind, Mother was a patron of Mrs Bloomer and when that particular garment billowed out in a stiff southerly it was almost as if mother herself had a grip on the clothesline and was madly trying to do a trapeze act on her own. If by chance I had some of my friends over to play on washing day, which was nearly every day with mother, I would quickly steer them around to the front of the house, out of sight of mum's personal washing limbering up or doing their trapeze act.

Another dislike of mine was that I hated wearing braces. They were an article of clothing which was popular in those days. Now mother was a sucker for sales. One day she went to a sale being held at Mrs McPhee's shop. The shop was seemingly stocked with miles of ribbons, millions of buttons, hair clips, lace, hand mirrors, corsets, variety goods, various articles of clothing and other goods too numerous to mention. That was where mother bought the four pairs of highly coloured braces for her four school-age sons. I hated braces and flatly refused to wear them.

It was father who had the final say, "Look here young man you'll wear them to school tomorrow do you hear?" I glowered at my father. "And if you don't" he added, "I'll tan your hide with them." So it was wear the braces or get a belting. Father never whacked his sons much and never the girls, but if he did they were occasions to remember and regret.

Next morning came and after father's departure for the timber yard and work, we started to get ready for school. I was the last to don my braces. Tommy was strutting around hooking his thumbs in his pair, making them snap. He had seen Mr Hare the auctioneer do that on auction days when he used to auction horses, cattle, pigs and various types of horse-drawn vehicles, among other items. Tommy sort of felt that it made him more adult than his fourteen years. Mother watched and felt my reluctance as I fumbled with the buttons on my school trousers. Mother was wise. She smiled at me gently and said softly, "Why don't you like wearing braces?" I stood head down, lips thrust out belligerently. "Come," mother added, "why don't you like wearing them?" I said truculently, "They make me look like a girl." Mother laughed and replied, "But other boys wear them." "That's them, I'm me," I muttered. Mother answered, "My boy, you certainly are you. Anyway Father said you have to wear them, so off you go all of you." We traipsed off together, strung out along the railway line which led to school.

Teddy and I walked slowly along behind the others. Somehow I had to get rid of my braces before I got' to school. I could see the other boys laughing at me and the thought was agonising to my twelve-year-old mind. But to me the grim prospect of sister Kathleen or Ethel Edna telling mother or father that I had not worn the braces was a strong possibility. I deliberately slowed my pace and Teddy did so accordingly. He was having a few practice shots with his index fingers. I knew I had to embroil Teddy in the braces removal operation. Besides, it meant that he too could share some of the guilt in disobeying father.

Teddy began shooting faster. It was then I had my idea. I watched Teddy reload his imaginary firearm and I prepared to put my plan into action. I patted my hip and said, "Well I ain't wearin' no gun today." "I am," replied Teddy, peering into a clump of teatree for an Indian. "I got a .44 and a .45." "You ain't," I said. "I have so," said Teddy. "You haven't," I said, "'cause you're wearin' braces and not a gun belt and cowboys don't wear braces they wear belts." Teddy gazed at his midriff and at his pants being held up by the braces. "Of course," I said, "we could take our braces off and tie 'em around our waist." Teddy in one of his rare practical moments replied, "No we'll only get into trouble from father." "No we won't," I insisted. "We'll still be wearin' 'em won't we?" And I hammered horne the final nail. "And you never see Cowboy Charlie wearin' braces do you?" I said. And assisting one another, we removed our braces. I breathed a sigh of relief. Honour was restored and with guns popping we ran heller skeller the remaining distance to school.

Once, during school hours, I thought I caught a disapproving look from sister Kathleen but little Ethel Edna never even noticed the change in our attire. I had it all planned. On the way horne after school, we would don our braces and no one would be any the wiser.

Freckles, Teddy and I didn't use the short cut horne but walked along the railway line which ran past our house. One of the two little wood-burning company engines was usually puffing up and down the railway line. They never travelled very fast. This day the one called Captain Stirling was chugging up the long quarter-mile slope, towing a length of empty jinkers for the timber yard to be loaded with timber. We knew all the firemen and the drivers. This day Captain Stirling was being driven by Mr Larry Meaghan. Father reckoned that Mr Larry Meaghan had been trying to get his engine driver's ticket for so long that the board of examiners gave it to him because of his persistence.

The railway engine drew level with Freckles, Teddy and I. We waved and shouted, "Gooday," to Mr Meaghan. Mr Meaghan shouted his reply, "How are you boys?" And Freckles yelled, "Give us a ride?" and Mr Larry Meaghan shouted more in fun than intent, "Jump on." I was the first to start running along the line of jinkers. "Corne on," I yelled and with a leap I jumped onto the flat-topped jinker parallel to me. The running Freckles leapt up beside me. Teddy was running fast and I yelled, "Grab hold of that iron post."

Now alongside each of the jinkers were removable steel stanchions which were placed there to keep the logs and milled timber in place. Teddy grabbed hold of one of the stanchions and attempted to pull himself up. As he was halfway up on the jinker the train jerked forward and Teddy lost his balance and slipped. He grabbed the stanchion for support and somehow his braces went over the stanchion and Teddy went over the side. Freckles and I looked on in horror.

There he was, his braces stretched to twice their usual length, anchoring him to the jinker, both his legs swinging and missing the wheels of the jinker by inches. I leapt forward in an attempt to help him by pulling him up onto the floor of the jinker. Then Teddy's braces broke and he tumbled rolling down the embankment away from the train.

Anyway Mr Larry Meaghan told father. Father came home from work grim faced and lined his two sons up. Teddy escaped unhurt and father admonished us both. But because the incident could have ended in tragedy, father was too shaken to give us a whacking. As far as I was concerned the incident turned out okay as none of us boys were compelled to wear braces again. In fact mother cut them up and father made belts out of them. You could trust mother to make sure she got her six shillings worth of value from them braces.

Chapter 18

Father was a great fight fan and his idol was Jack Dempsey. When Dempsey lost what has been called the Battle of the Long Count against Gene Tunney, father was inconsolable. I followed father's interest in boxing and because of this I was always chosen to read the news out of the newspaper to father. Especially the boxing news. Father didn't care much for Jack Johnson. He maintained that Johnson lowered the prestige of black boxers. I thought mother's assessment of Jack Johnson was fair. She said it was just the press and people, white people getting back at Johnson because he was black.

Father had been a good boxer himself in his youth. In fact he was a good all round sportsman. He used to don the gloves with us boys and show us how to throw or block a punch. If any of us boys adopted the crouching style of more modern day boxers father would quickly point out it was wrong by throwing a stinging uppercut to prove he was right.

Myalup was the name of a sustenance camp where men were employed in a government scheme, digging irrigation ditches so as to alleviate unemployment. Myalup was about eighteen kilometres from Yarloop and ten kilometres out of Harvey.

From the three places men were asked to take part in a boxing tournament. Father became the trainer of the four men chosen to represent Yarloop. For four weeks, three nights a week, father would come home from the shed where they used to train on Mr Kattak's property, smelling heavily of liniment embrocation. Harold, Teddy and I always went along to training nights and we used to come home (much to mother's disgust) smelling of the embrocation almost as much as father. Father said that Billy Wellington (who used to fight light-weight) was Yarloop's best chance of victory. He also maintained that Billy had the making of a champion.

The night of the tournament came and the Yarloop hall, come picture theatre, come dance hall, come boxing stadium, was packed. A boxing ring had been erected at the rear of the hall. Billy Wellington's bout was listed as the main fight of the evening. Of the three preceding bouts, Yarloop had won two and lost one.

At last the time came for the main fight and blood-thirsty me had wormed my way ringside. The bell rang (they had borrowed it from the school) signifying the start of the first round. Billy Wellington's opponent came out peeking between his gloves. Billy let go a lightning right-hand which sent his opponent reeling back against the ropes. Then Billy swarmed all over him. The referee jumped in between the two boxers and declared Billy Wellington the winner. Father said later that the bout could go down as one of the shortest in boxing history.

During the potato digging seasons, which were March and October, father would go potato digging on weekends to augment the family income. Tommy, Harold and I went along to pick up and bag the potatoes for father as he dug them - at least until the March flies, big and vicious, bit us, then we would go down to the little creek which ran down between the potato fields and bathe our fIy-stung limbs in the clear cold water. Sometimes we would catch minnows or hunt for giIgies. The man who owned the potato patch always gave father a half bag of potatoes to take horne and our little band would start for horne in the growing darkness.

The smell of wood smoke from mother's wood stove, the tall lamps glowing through the window and the delicious smell of mother's evening meal never failed to make us quicken our steps. It was times such as this, when father and his sons stepped through the door, that we realized unconsciously or otherwise what horne and family togetherness truly meant.

Chapter 19

As a family we relied a lot upon the bush to help replenish the family larder. On some weekends father would go out into the swamp country west of town and bring home a brace or two of wild duck or into the hill country east to hunt for kangaroo or emu. But our favourite hunt was pig hunting. The Darling Range country of Yarloop was beautiful country and the hills were moulded into valleys and verdant hollows. Some were only a few hundred yards across while others were over a mile wide. The floors of these valleys were always a mass of vegetation, acres of paperbark, bulrush and wiregrass. This then was the habitat of the wild pig. Domesticated pigs are short sighted and not very good at hearing, but their feral counterparts are just the opposite. They are also very agile and fitted into their transplanted environment perfectly.

No pig dog ever killed a wild boar, but a good dog could always hold a boar at bay. Our pig dog was a bitza, half bull terrier, half collie. He had the bull terrier strength of jaw and the grace and speed of the border collie. One of father's workmates owned a horse and cart. He had only been in Australia a few years. Father said he was a likeable little bloke and he had taken Geordie out on a few hunting trips and Geordie said those trips were really something. One day father suggested that they go on a pig hunt together. It was a good twenty mile drive up into the ranges and into pig country. Early on this Saturday morning Geordie drove up the sandy track where Teddy interned his imaginary Indians.

Father decided to let us three older boys accompany him; that was Tommy, Harold and myself. As it meant a night out in the bush we had to take cooking and camping gear along with us. This was loaded on the cart. So father, with his three sons along with Geordie, climbed aboard and with much waving from the remainder of the family and cries of good hunting, except from Teddy who was sulking because he was not included in the party, we made our way parallel to the railway line which led into the hills.

It was half an hour before sunset when we reached our destination. The kookaburras had begun their evening laughing call and a wave of black cockatoos flew overhead. Magpies could be heard calling their familiar "Look-out, look-out" call further down the valley. After finding a suitable spot father left Geordie, Harold and I to set up camp while he and Tommy went looking for pig sign. Geordie hobbled the horse out and us two boys began cutting and carting blackboy rush for bedding while Geordie made the fire. He placed the big black billycan of water on the fire, on top of the blaze. It capsized and doused the fire. We laughed at his effort and Harold said, "You'll have to make the fire in another place now Mr Donaldson 'cause the ground is all wet and father will want to make a damper in the ashes for supper." Geordie gathered an armful of fresh dry wood and replied, "What do you mean, damper?" Harold explained the process and I muttered, "Now I know what pommy means."

Father and Tommy returned and they were jubilant. They had found some sign a quarter of a mile down the valley. "Fresh too," said father. "Water still muddy in their tracks, I reckon they must have heard us. They won't go far and with a bit of luck we should catch up with them in the morning." Tommy began peeling potatoes and onions and cutting up bacon and with sausages he put the lot in the camp oven on the fire. Father put flour in a dish and adding baking powder and water, mixed it into a firm dough, while Geordie watched fascinated. Father scraped a depression in the hot ashes and he laid the flattened dough carefully in the makeshift oven. Geordie squatted on his heels and said, "You mean we're going to eat that Bill?" Father laughed and replied, "Well if you don't you're going to go hungry."

After about twenty minutes father broke a bush and removing the now cooked damper from the ashes, dusted it rigorously, and there it lay cooked to a beautiful crisp white and brown. "Well," said Geordie, "that really is something." Tommy ladled out the stew broke the damper, handing a piece to Geordie and to each of us. Geordie bit into his piece tentatively. Father and us boys watched him with amusement. "Well," said father with a grin, "what's the verdict?" Geordie gave a yell and replied, "It's even better than bread." Tommy said with a laugh, "We'll make a bushman out of you yet Mr Donaldson." The damper and the stew quickly diminished. That night we lay under a million stars and we talked. Geordie told us of his home in faraway England and how he used to work long hours in the coal mines when a boy and how he had worked his way out to Australia on a ship as a stoker. The last thing I heard was Tommy saying to father, "The wind's in the right direction." Then I was asleep.

Next morning we rose early and breakfasted before sunrise. Though the morning sun had sent its rays into the sky to the east of us the valley was still in shadow. Gyp was trembling with excitement. Once he barked and Harold clouted him into silence. We made our way down the valley. It was a cool morning and the day was cloudy. Father tested the wind with a wet forefinger. He carried his short-barrelled .303, Tommy had the double-barrel shotgun, while Geordie had father's long-barrel .303. Harold and I carried a hunting knife each. We strung out in a line, Tommy taking the lead while Harold brought up the rear. He kept stopping for wattle gum, and father told him to stop eating it because it would give him a guts ache.

We had walked about a half mile. The ground had become boggy and the vegetation, consisting of bulrush and wiregrass, became thicker. We slipped and slid forward in attempts to keep on the kwokka and pig pads which criss-crossed our path and father warned Tommy and Geordie to keep the safety catch on their weapons. Gyp was in front, eager and excited, and Tommy had to keep calling him to heel. Suddenly father stopped and raised his hand. He pointed groundward and there were several sets of fresh tracks leading away from us. Father whispered, "About ten of them, probably a sow, a boar and several young ones and don't shoot the boar or the sow. Go for the biggest of the young." And he added for Geordie's information, "Shoot for behind the ears." Tommy was a good shot and knew where to aim.

Father leant and patted Gyp and said, "Find 'em boy." They were the words he had waited for. With a whine he ran forward, nose to the ground in a lithe crouching run. Father, Tommy and Geordie moved forward parallel to one another.

Then there came a crashing in the undergrowth and the heavy barking of Gyp. The dog was a good 200 yards to the left of them. The hunters quickened their pace. There was a crash to the right of them and the boomer came towards them leaping high. Geordie raised his rifle, more out of reflex, and father shouted to him, "No, let him go."

The big grey kangaroo veered away from them leaping high to clear the vegetation. We suddenly came out into a clearing. Here the bulrush and wiregrass was that high it fell down and made a carpet over the water. Gyp was barking, moving forward with a crouching more like a eat's than a dog-footed run. The pigs were under the carpet of vegetation with Gyp on top.

Then we saw the old man boar. He was enormous. A real razorback. His six-inch tusks curled up above his snout. He had come out from under the carpet of bulrush and wiregrass first and stood in defiance on the patch of higher ground where we were grouped. He stood with legs apart, head thrust forward. Gyp reached solid ground and the boar lunged toward him. Gyp spun away sideways and the razor-sharp tusks missed him by a whisker. Then the sow and the young pigs broke through the carpet of green and partly submerged paperbark trees. The boar saw his mob and, grunting with rage he rushed toward our dog. Gyp ran toward the sow and her young. Father saw the black and white half grown boar. He brought his rifle up to his shoulder and squeezed the trigger.

The young pig was flung sideways by the impact of the bullet and was dead before he hit the ground. Geordie fired and missed. Tommy let go with the shotgun and the impact of shot caught one of the piglets square and it dropped dead. Geordie cursed and pumped another cartridge into the chamber of his .303. It was then the old man boar decided on more direct action.

With a squeal he came at the group of hunters. Father roared, "Run tree tree." Nobody had to be told twice. With a yell I ran to the nearest paperbark tree and began to climb. Luckily paperbarks are easy to climb with many jutting branches. Harold threw down .his knife and attempted to climb over the top of me. Father sprang behind a water-rotted stump. Father said later Geordie was even better than the Galilean because he actually *ran* over the water. Tommy jumped into the limbs of a fallen, partly submerged paperbark. Geordie could feel the tusks of that old man boar tickling the calves of his legs.

It was then Gyp came to the rescue. He raced past the flying Geordie and the boar then he came back with a rush. He sidestepped the boar, flashed back in and his bull terrier-like jaws fastened on to one of the ears of the pig, who came to a slithering halt.

The boar squealed with rage and flung his body in an arc in an effort to dislodge his adversary. But Gyp hung on. Father ran forward and aimed his rifle at the boar. But the pig and dog were a cartwheeling mass of fury and father could not shoot because he was afraid of hitting Gyp, and he knew the dog would not let go his ear-hold. Besides, father hated shooting animals when there was no need to do so. It was then that Tommy yelled, "Get a stick and clout him one." Meaning of course the pig.

Tommy put his shotgun down and broke a limb from his haven, the paperbark, and threw it to father. Father picked up the stick, ran up beside the fighting animals and brought the stick down with a mighty whack on the back of that old man boar. The stick being rotten, it broke and father was carried forward by the amount of swing he put into the blow. He sprawled forward and fell right on top of the dog and pig.

Gyp must have got a shock to see father join in the fray. Because he let go of the pig's ear then rolled away, then onto his feet. For one or two frozen seconds man and boar lay side by side. Then father and that old man boar became galvanized into action. Father leapt to his feet and ran one way, and that old razorback he got up and ran the other. Gyp started out after him but Tommy called him back. It was Geordie humour that restored us to normality as our guest yelled out from the safety of his tree, "Eh Bill, you're whiter than I am." Father muttered a reply which sounded like, "You pommy so and so."

Chapter 20

The huge jarrah tree which stood a hundred metres from our house was a real wonder of nature. It took 32 of my boyish steps to circle its sprawling girth. Years of storms had trimmed the growth of its branches, but it reared sixty metres into the blue of the sky. Year after year the kookaburras and the magpies nested and reared their offspring in the hollows of the lofty branches and we always had scraps of food for the succession of each new colony every year. There was always some reminder of me and my brothers and sisters around the tree. Scratch marks in the hoary old bark and all the odds and ends of children at play scattered around it.

I remember my baby brother, who was temporarily in my care, spied a large green caterpillar crawling in one of the folds of bark on the forest giant. From my shoulder he reached out with one small greedy hand and popped the caterpillar in his mouth. My hundred-metres-away yell brought mother from the house with a rush. She promptly rescued the caterpillar and baby Frank from probable asphyxiation. Then in fright she attempted to slap me across the ear into the bargain. When mother made a sweep at us kids the clip always had a round arm approach which gave us plenty of time to duck. Knowing the technique, I evaded the one over the caterpillar.

Father was a first class shot with a rifle and he was the proud owner of two beautifully kept .303 rifles. Occasionally he would take the rifles down from the racks, polish, repolish, clean and reclean them. He would invariably challenge mother to a shooting contest. Mother herself, from the resting position, was almost as good a shot as father. If mother accepted the challenge, a bottle would be placed in one of the folds of the old jarrah tree and the contest would begin. Father, nine times out of ten, would shoot and snap off the neck of the bottle, then mother would try for the centre of the target. Father would then shatter the base of the bottle.

Now mother was an avid picture fan and pictures were held once a week in Yarloop. That week's show was *The King of Kings*. Money for the flicks in those days was scarce and especially hard to find if you were a member of a large family like ours. But mother was shrewd and often put it over father without him knowing. This occasion was one of them. But it did turn out differently.

In the days of silent films, pictures could be rather dull if you could not read the dialogue. As mother could neither read nor write and I was considered the quickest if not the best reader, although I was the fourth eldest in our family, I therefore invariably accompanied mother on her occasional picture nights.

In the silent era, the movies, or flicks as they were called, were always of a three to four hours duration. First would be the Pathe news or gazette (of course weeks old) then there would be a comedy. There would then be a half-hour break, which gave the film operator time to change reels. Then the main attraction would commence. Mother and I always arrived at the flicks early so we could get a good seat, which was usually in the centre of the hall. Mother always made sure I went to the toilet before the commencement of the film because she didn't want any break in the reading of the subtitles.

Mother's favourite actress was Marie Dressler. I think it was because she was such a motherly figure that mother felt empathy towards her. When poor Marie was hard done by mother would wipe a tear from her eye. Her favourite actor was swashbuckling Douglas Fairbanks, while my favourite actors were the cowboy heroes such as Tom Mix, Buck Jones and Fred Thompson. There wasn't much dialogue in the cowboy pictures. They mainly consisted of galloping horses and popping guns, so the story line could be followed fairly easy. Just as well because I would be cheering on my cowboy hero and mother of course would be cheering along with me.

Getting back to the rifles, shooting of course, to father, was a man's sport and male-like, he disliked being beaten by a member of the so called weaker sex at anything, and of all things, shooting. Unthinkable!

The day of the contest-to-be came. Though father didn't know there was going to be one, because they were usually of a spontaneous nature. Just before father came home from work at five in the afternoon, mother instructed me to fill the target bottle with almost-boiling water. She then tightly sealed the bottle and I placed it in the open oven of the kitchen stove. Mother then placed the two rifles on the verandah table. As soon as father walked on to the verandah she called out from the kitchen, "I've got the rifles ready, Bill. Feel like a challenge?"

"I feel a bit tired," father replied, then added, "Okay, you're on." Then he put his big number nine foot on the edge of mother's snare and said, "What's the bet?" Mother tightened the noose a little, not daring to look at me hovering near the open oven door. "Well," mother replied, "you let me have two shots and if I break the bottle completely, I'm going to see *The King of Kings* on Saturday night." Unable to contain myself any longer I piped up, "Yes mother, don't forget I'm coming as your reader." "It's a bet," said father cheerfully, and to me, "Go and put a bottle on the tree."

The two contestants stepped off the verandah; father in his dungarees and flannel shirt; mother, house frock and apron attired. I turned and scooped the almost red hot bottle from the interior of the oven. Mother had already placed a kitchen chair outside, to rest her rifle on. But father scorned a resting shot. As I ran past them, juggling the red hot bottle, mother implored with unconscious reverence, "Don't for God's sake drop it." I thought with equal piety, "Sure enough for *The King of Kings* sake I won't."

I placed the bottle in the usual fold in the old forest giant. By this time the rest of the children were grouped behind the two contestants. The girls with fingers in their ears in preparation for the crack of the rifles and the boys calling out encouragement, yet still trying to remain impartial. Mother waited until I came back from the tree and joined the other children. Then I almost muffed the whole thing. As mother brought her rifle up in perfect line with the red bottle, gleaming in the western rays of the sun, I stepped within half a metre of her. The gentle pressure of her index finger on the trigger coincided with my movement and the shot rang out.

Mother stared in disbelief at the unmarked target, then made one of her round arm swipes at me and, because I too was staring at the bottle, the clip in the ear this time was successful. The rest of the family, still divided and impartial, groaned their oohs and aahs, and father, well he just roared with laughter. At that moment I felt like turning traitor and barracking for father on the off chance he would let me go and see the flicks anyway. But I thought better of it.

Mother looked at father grimly and said, "Anyway I've still got one shot left." He looked at mother and saw the gleam of tears of disappointment in her eyes. She angrily jerked her chair into a new position and resting her rifle on the chair back took careful aim. By this time the suspense was almost too much for me. I was now safely ensconced on the verandah.

It was from there I saw it all happen and 1 will never be able to explain the wonder of it. Mother always squeezed the trigger as a good shot should do. As the pressure of her index finger on the trigger reached the point of no return, father with the quick easy flow of movement born of years of practice, brought his rifle to his shoulder and pressed the trigger. The two shots blended in perfect unison and the echo reverberated through the bush. The bottle exploded into smithereens and mother sprang to her feet and yelled with excitement, "I did it Billy, I did it."

Father, in seconds, had his rifle cradled in his arms. He looked at mother and said gruffly, "Good shot love, a darn good shot. Now eject the shell and after we have had supper I'll clean your rifle for you." My father was not the king of kings, but to me, a ten-year-old boy, on that day, he really was a king among men and we did see the movie. Mother and I together.

Chapter 21

Father was a self-taught leather worker. He could mend harness, plait whips and make belts. He was an excellent cobbler and always mended his and mother's footwear. His size nine working boots took a lot of hard wear and in their old age they had been regularly mended. It was a Friday morning that mother drew father's attention to the dilapidated condition of his working boots. "I know they're just about beyond repair, but they'll have to last a little longer," father replied. Mother shook her head emphatically and said, "I'm going to get you a new pair and that's that." Father grinned and replied "What will you use for money?" Mother answered, "I'll see Mrs McPhee and ask if she will book me up a pair."

Mrs McPhee was the owner of one of the two stores in the town. The other being owned by the timber company. Mrs McPhee was sixty years old and she ran the little store on her own. Mother used to make a few extra scones or cakes and send them down to her occasionally with sister Kathleen or Ethel

Edna. She couldn't trust us boys with such goodies. Mother was shrewd. She knew her small gifts would eventually payoff.

Father got ready for work the following day, Saturday morning. The mill worker worked half a day on Saturdays. Father gave an extra wince as he pulled on the boots. I believe that wince was for mother's benefit. After father had departed mother donned her best dress and, promising us kids dire retribution on any mischief, she departed on the half-kilometre walk to Mrs McPhee's store. Us kids made optimistic bets on the likelihood of mother getting the boots. An hour later Teddy, who had been shooting a couple of stray Indians, brought us all out of the house with a yell to see mother walking up the railway line with a huge brown paper parcel clutched in her arms. Mother deposited the parcel and other smaller ones on the kitchen table and out of the barrage of questions and complaints she said, "Yes, that's Father's boots," and pointing to the other packages she continued, "and that's bicarbonate of soda, that's cream of tartar and that's dried fruit." To Harold she said, "You go and ask Mrs Dann to let me have a dozen eggs and I'll pay her on pay day."

Then with an air of quiet dramatics she produced a packet of boiled sweets from her handbag and began to share them equally among her clamouring children. Mother said, "I'm going to make a nice cake for Mrs McPhee." And pointing at Ethel Edna, "You can take it down to her on your way to school on Monday." At Ethel Edna's wail, "But I'll be late for school," mother added, "And you can lick the cake tin out after I've made this cake." Ethel Edna was satisfied. Mother told Tommy where to place father's new boots, under her and father's bed and she said, "Not a word about the boots to Father." The 11.30 Saturday knock-off whistle blew. The children all stood around in strategic positions near the bedroom door. How do you keep secrets with children?

Mother, who was busy at the stove, looked at us kids, groaned and said, "Now you all get out the back door and play, right this minute, before your Father comes home." We trooped out into the back yard just as father walked in. I was the last to leave. I leapt down the steps arms akimbo and said, "Gee Father you sure have got a big foot." Father, not wanting to spoil what he sensed was mother's surprise said, "What does he mean?" Mother rushed outside, dish cloth raised menacingly, "Didn't I tell you to go and play?" "Yes mother," I replied, "right this minute Mother." Mother walked back inside and entered the bedroom where father was sitting and said to him, "Your new boots are under the bed." Father reached down and retrieved the parcel and unwrapping it gazed at his new boots with admiration. He looked at mother and said simply, "Thanks Mother." And that was mother's moment of happiness.

Chapter 22

It was after supper and the family all sat around the huge open fireplace. Father turned and lowered the wick on the tall kerosene lamp which illuminated the room. He then lit his pipe with a coal from the open fire, picking it up expertly in timber calloused fingers. He sat back in his chair and puffing luxuriantly on his pipe he said, "You know Mother, those new boots you bought me put me in mind of an incident on a station I worked on up north." He winked at mother, "You kids want to hear it?"

There was an affirmative chorus and father said, "I was about twenty years old at the time and the boss told me to ride the south boundary fence and look for breaks. I had an elderly Aboriginal called Waladi with me, who was a good stockman and good company. We had a packhorse to carry our provisions and camping gear.

"It was summer and the day was hot and sultry. We had made an early start and by midday, we were some ten miles from the homestead. We had found a few breaks in the boundary fence. Mainly caused by kangaroos and emus. Sometimes we would have to pull away the carcasses of emus which in their stupidity had become tangled in the fence and perished.

"We came to a wide dry creek which the boundary fence crossed. The fence from one bank to another spanning a distance of about 30 yards was down, evidently from a previous flash flood, and was also heaped intermittently with debris. We stripped our horses of their gear and after watering them at a nearby pool, we had lunch of cold meat and bread then began work, to reconstruct the fence. It was Waladi who drew my attention to the long line of black cloud in the east. He pointed with his chin and said tersely, 'Yoongoo comin'.' Which translated," said father with a grin, "meant rain. I replied, 'Big one?' 'Must be: he said in the Aboriginal way. 'Well we're nearly finished: I said, and as I tied up the last few strands of wire, Waladi saddled the horses.

"The black belt of cloud now covered a third of the eastern sky. We knew of a cave which was about a quarter of a mile from us and situated about a hundred yards away from the fence. It had always been a favourite camping place for boundary riders and musterers. We urged our horses forward right into the approaching storm. The air had become still and the birds had fled or taken refuge. We came to the cave. It was enormous, large enough to shelter our three horses and ourselves. And then the storm was upon us.

"To say the thunder rolled and the lightning flashed would not be enough," father said. "For long minutes the thunder was a continual roll of ear numbing sound and the lightning sprayed flashes of light into the cave. And its flashing brought the many cave paintings into almost three dimensional relief. Old Waladi's eyes, and no doubt mine, shone white between the purple and orange flashes of lightning. The rain came down in a continuous stream. Our horses, wise in the ways of the weather, stood patiently, hips down, as if knowing that the rain meant green pastures.

"Then the rain stopped almost as quick as it had started. We walked to the cave's entrance and gazed at the beautiful brown flood of water which tumbled down the hills. Waladi looked at me, grinned and said, 'That fence down again across the river.' I grinned back at him using the Aboriginal vernacular, 'Must be,' and we both laughed. 'Could be south wind tomorrow, cattle all come up the river,' Waladi said. 'Yes,' I replied, 'we might as well go back to the homestead and tell the boss what happened.'

"What did the boss say?" interjected Harold. "Just hang on a bit," said father, "I haven't finished yet. Anyway, as we had been riding on the opposite side of the fence it meant we had to cut the fence to get back on to our own side." I piped up, "But Father, what was you doing on the wrong side of the fence?" "Because," said Tommy, "the cave was on that side and they had to use it for shelter, ain't that right Father?" "Yes," said father, "that's right. Anyway, as I was saying before I was rudely interrupted, we rode over to the fence, dismounted and began removing the top wire from the strainer post. The thunder, still grumbling, was moving away from us but there was still some vicious stabs of lightning to the west.

"The fence wire was number ten wire which is pretty tough. But the usual pliers done the job. I removed three strands of wire, leaving the bottom three still tied to the strainer, and the horses stepped neatly over. Waladi threaded the cut wire back to the strainer post. We pulled and tied two strands tight, then started on the last thread of wire. The top one.

"It was then the lightning struck. I was at the end of the wire pulling with the pliers. I acted as the earth. It was all so unbelievably sudden. So unsuspected and instant. I was flung on my back with a feeling of pain in the stomach as if I had been punched. Waladi was knocked sideways sprawling and a curious thing happened. As he fell one of his boots went flying off his foot. Looking back on what happened I believe Waladi would have been electrocuted if he had been wearing socks, but our feet were dry. Thanks to the cave. Anyway, we tied the top wire and cut across country to the homestead and when we got there the river was in flood and we had to swim our horses across it."

I looked at my father and said, "Gee Father, you know you should get that all written down." He looked at me quizzically and said, "Maybe one of you kids will one day write it for me." And so I did.

Chapter 23

Mother only had one tribal sister and had not seen her for ten years. So one day she said to father she wanted to pay her a visit. Aunty Maude was married and lived in Brookton, a little town in the wheat belt on the great southern railway, some 330 kilometres from Yarloop. Mother was gone for two weeks and father had his hands full while mother was away. Though us older children looked after the younger ones, father had to work, then come home to help and supervise the activities of his brood, especially when it came to cooking and serving meals. For the two weeks during mother's absence, we lived on stews, because that was the only meal father could successfully cook.

We were all pleased when mother came home. As she stepped through the door, and after hugs and kisses, a boy of my age sidled through the door behind her. He was Aunty Maude's eldest son Gerry. It was the first time we ever had a relation visit us and we were all thrilled to see him. Especially us boys. He didn't come to school the next day as mother reasoned he was too tired after their long train journey from Brookton. But the following day he trooped off to school with the rest of us. Gerry was my age, twelve years old, a handsome boy and all the girls at school admired him. His lazy manner was deceptive, for he proved to be the fastest runner and best high jumper at school, much to Terry Wilkins' disgust because he had been the fastest runner before Gerry came to school. One day he called Gerry "skinny black legs" and offered to fight him.

My cousin was reluctant to fight, but with encouragement from Freckles and I, he accepted the challenge. A crowd of boys and a few girls followed the two combatants to the flat ground at the back of the infant schoolroom, an area where most of the fights were settled. The two boys were evenly matched in size, though Terry Wilkins was a year older. They shaped up, Terry made a wild roundabout swing at Gerry and missed. Gerry in turn made a wild swing at Terry and clouted him on the side of the head. Terry jumped backwards and shouted, "Ow, my ear." "Have you had enough?" I said to Terry. "Yes," he replied. That one fight elevated Gerry's standing at school, and when it came to fighting, the boys in his age group left him alone.

The weekend came and it was hot. So grabbing a pair of bathers, finding a spare pair for Gerry and getting permission from mother, we went for a swim. The swimming pool at Yarloop was in the Logan Brook. It was a delightful spot, the banks were lined with blue clay and clover grew profusely along the edges. Trees lined the banks, with weeping willows dipping their branches and gently moving in the current. Tom tits, robins and other bird life fluttered throughout the trees and gilgies lurked and minnows swam in the clear water.

A small waterfall was at the head of the swimming pool and water cascaded down from the neck of the brook and tumbled into the wider pool itself. Some twenty metres of the pool was over four metres deep. This day, to Teddy and I, was of added interest because we wanted to show Gerry the swimming pool and also show him our prowess in the water. It never dawned on us to ask Gerry if he could swim or not. As far as we were concerned we just assumed that being our age he naturally could swim.

We stood on the bank of the swimming pool and pointed the deep parts out and which parts it was safe to dive in. Then with a wild yell Teddy and I dived into the water. I swam the twenty metres up to the waterfall and called out to my reluctant cousin, "Come on, get in, it's beaut." Gerry without any more hesitation dived in. In fact he didn't dive, he landed flat on his stomach, then almost immediately disappeared below the surface of the water. He rose to the surface and began thrashing the water with his arms and legs. He sank again, then upon rising to the surface began to dog paddle. Just enough to keep his nose and mouth out of the water.

From the rocky ledge at the waterfall I yelled out to him to turn back. But he kept dog paddling toward me and the falls. At last, gasping, spluttering and breathing heavily, he reached the waterfall. He looked at me and Teddy in triumph and between breaths said, "There you are, you blokes thought I couldn't swim." And so as he could keep his boyish pride intact, I hadn't the heart to tell him he couldn't. Before he went back to Brookton at the end of summer he could swim and dive as well as any of us.

Chapter 24

Living in a timber mill town like Yarloop we always saw the finished product of sawn timber stacked in the huge timber yard. There were thousands of metres of all dimensions. As a boy I never really thought of timber as being trees. At least not until the day that all the children of the sixth, seventh and eighth grades at school were taken on an excursion to Nanga Brook by one of the little railway engines used by Millars. They were small compared to the huge C class locomotives owned by the government railways. But they were powerful and pulled and pushed hundreds of tonnes of timber down from the Darling Ranges from places like Nanga Brook and Hoffman. This day thirty children from school packed into the railway vans and we chugged the 28 kilometres to Nanga Brook.

Arriving at midday, everybody unpacked and shared or partially exchanged lunches. After partaking of our midday meal we walked some distance into the bush to where the fallers were falling the huge jarrah giants. This was before the days of power saws and the crosscut saw was still in use. The tree would be scarfed, that is, partly cut into with axes wielded by the fallers and these men were poetry in motion. The fluidity of the individual strokes of their axes was timed to perfection. As soon as one axe sank into the tree and was withdrawn, the other would bite into the vacated space. When the scarf was considered large enough, the Symonds crosscut would go into action. With a push, pull, pull, push motion, the saw would gradually sink into the tree trunk.

For some undefined reason within me, I felt sad. But being merely twelve years old, I could not explain in words the hurtful finality of what I was about to witness. The saw seemed to sing as it bit into the tree. Spurts of sawdust flew out from either side of the ever deepening cut. The fallers did not pause. This was their work. Honed to perfection, they were experts at their trade. Imperceptibly the forest giant began to bow her head. The fallers with one accord stopped, removed the saw and stepped back.

For long seconds she began her inevitable return to earth. Then with a headlong rush she passed the point of balance and with a mighty whoosh of sound, crashed to earth, sending dust and scattered undergrowth into the air. Then when the dust and branches had settled, the children ran to the fallen giant to examine her more closely. But there was a sadness in me. Somehow I felt the tree had been killed and I knew it was gone forever.

Chapter 25

The year 1929 came and with it the worldwide Depression. Sometimes men out of work and carrying their swags would knock on our door looking for handouts of food. As we lived not far from the main road into Yarloop, these visitors were frequent. Mother always had a loaf of bread and a small pot of honey or homemade jam for these men who could not find employment. Most people in Yarloop felt that the Depression would not affect the timber industry, reasoning that timber would always be needed for houses and other buildings.

Life in our community continued as before, but there were ominous signs of the Depression in the air. Father would come home from work grim faced, and tell mother the names of the men who had been laid off from the mill. As the Depression worsened, we could see more and more men carrying their swags and tramping along the roads. Us children used to call them tramps. One day when doing some shopping for mother I saw a tramp gazing into the bakery window. After purchasing mother's goods, I had sixpence change which I offered to the tramp. He thanked me and went into the baker's shop and purchased a loaf of bread. Upon my arriving home, mother asked for her change. Then I told her what I had done with it. She looked at me with something between a smile and a frown. She chided me gently then. Not about giving away sixpence, but for talking to a stranger.

All the Davis children had good voices, which we inherited from mother and father. Though neither' of them could read or write they knew most of the popular music hall songs of the day. Father was a tenor and mother a contralto and many evenings we sat around the open fireplace in winter singing together, our faces lit by the glow of firelight. But of all the good voices in our family Kathleen's voice was the best. She had the ability to make people weep when they heard her sing, and was always in demand at concerts. Sometimes she sang at half time during the local silent picture shows. She also sang in neighbouring towns such as Harvey and Waroona.

One of her favourite songs was called, *Won't You Buy My Pretty Flowers?* and one had only to look at the faces of the audience to see the effect her voice had on them. I can still see her standing centre stage, dressed in white, her long dark hair held back and tied in place with a bow. Sometimes at home during play she would dress up in one of mother's dresses, shoes and hat. Us kids, those of us who were available, would be her audience and she would sing for us. Then we would give her play money as payment.

The main waste product from the mill was sawdust. Timber such as scantlings were fed into the massive Cornish boiler which generated steam to turn the huge circular saws to cut the timber. The sawdust was carried away in overhead chutes and under air pressure was blown onto the sawdust heap some 150 metres from the mill. It was forever burning, and it often became a playground for us, the mill children.

Sometimes we would cadge potatoes from our mothers and roast them in the smouldering sawdust. Here we were able to let our imaginations run riot. There us boys played Cowboys and Indians and Cops and Robbers. Sometimes Kathleen would join in with us, but her favourite pastime was building castles out of pieces of timber and the damp sawdust. With the help of her younger sisters, she would build roads and bridges and manufacture little gardens made out of wild flowers and green bushes plucked from the side of the sawdust heap. Then she would give each garden a name such as Princess garden or Queen's garden, whatever took her fancy. This winter's day of 1932, Kathleen, myself, Teddy and Ethel Edna ran, played and somersaulted in the sawdust. It was deliciously damp and soft under our scurrying feet.

A week later Kathleen and Ethel Edna were in the local hospital with pneumonia. In those days it was an illness which had to run its course. This was long before penicillin and for four days the doctor fought the illness with all the knowledge that he had. Mother and father spent hours down at the hospital. At last came the turning point in the two girls' illnesses. Mother and father came home and told us the good news, they were both on the mend.

Father had offered to shave one or two of the patients in the men's ward and he was busy stropping his razor. Harold, Teddy and I were playing cricket in the back yard. We looked up to see one of the nurses running up the railway line. Harold ran inside and told mother and father. Father ran down the railway line to meet the nurse, who told him Kathleen had had a relapse.

Mother quickly followed father down to the hospital. The afternoon wore on and night fell. Us older boys gave the younger children something to eat and then put them to bed. Around ten o'clock mother and father stepped through the door. Their faces were stricken. To this day I remember father speaking in a low, strangled voice as he said, "Kathleen is dead."

Looking back through the years it seems as if mother was stronger than father in our grief. He seemed to grow older overnight. Ethel Edna recovered and came home a few days later. The town and district were shocked at Kathleen's death and the little church and cemetery were packed with mourners. Many openly wept in the realization that her beautiful fourteen-year-old voice was stilled forever.

One of the most difficult tasks mother and father had to face was to tell Ethel Edna that her sister was not coming home. Kathleen's death had been kept from her because she was recuperating from her own fight with pneumonia.

It was three days after the funeral. I was the first home from school that day. I walked into the kitchen where mother was peeling vegetables and she murmured, more to herself than to me, "Who's going to tell her?" I replied, "I will Mother." She looked at me and slowly nodded her head. I walked into Ethel's bedroom and leaning over her I said quickly, "Do you know Kath has gone to heaven?" The little eight-year-old girl stared at me and answered, "Does that mean we won't see her again?" I choked up and nodded my head. As I turned to walk away mother entered the bedroom and placed her arms around the softly weeping child, and the three of us cried together.

Mother had packed most of Kathleen's personal things away in a box high on a shelf. Such as her cuttings of film stars and dresses from the Ladies Home Journal, an imitation necklace, a pair of earrings and some of her school books.

Sometimes mother would take the box down and rearrange things and she would surreptitiously shed a silent tear.

One day father gently admonished her about her habit of taking the box down and told mother quietly that it would be better to give Kathleen's things to Ethel Edna. Mother replied, "But this is all 1 have left of her." "I know," gently replied father, "but we all have to accept the fact that she is no longer with us and go on living." So Kathleen's things, such as her imitation necklace, her earrings and other items were given to Ethel Edna who was now the eldest girl in the family.

Chapter 26

Mother was equally as good as father at telling stories. She used to call her stories true make-up stories. One of our favourites was about Kangaroo Kate. "Now Kangaroo Kate," mother would solemnly say, "was a waif, a stray, who had no mother and father and she used to work for this mean stingy couple. They made her work from daylight to dark. She used to have to wash the dishes, sweep the floor, shop and bring in the fire wood and wash the clothes. Oh they were very cruel people and they never paid her any wages. She only had one day off a week and on this day off she would go walking in the hills.

"One day she ventured further into the hills than she had done before and came upon this green valley and the valley was full of beautiful flowers and she came to this pool and the kangaroos were all lying about in the shade. Kate crept up closer to the resting kangaroos, but unknown to Kate, Mother Doe Kangaroo saw her and said, 'What are you creeping up on us for?' 'Oh; said Kate, 'I am lonely and unhappy.' 'Why are you unhappy?' said Mother Doe, 'Because; said Kate, 'my master and mistress are cruel to me and I don't want to live with them anymore, but I have nowhere to go.' 'Oh you poor little girl; said Mother Doe, 'I think you had better come and live with us.' So Kate lived with the kangaroos and if you can find that little valley you will see Kangaroo Kate running fleet footed with the kangaroos. Some people say they have seen her but nobody has any definite proof. She lives with the kangaroos all right, and she lived happily ever after."

Another one of mother's stories was about the kitchen. One night she got out of bed - she thought she heard voices in the kitchen, She tiptoed to the kitchen door. At this point in the story mother would solemnly say, "First the kettle was arguing with the teapot. 'Yes; said the kettle, 'I am the most important one in this kitchen because 1 hold the water.' 'You are not; retorted the teapot. 'Without me nobody could have a cup of tea.' 'No I am; said the frying pan. 'Without me nobody could have bacon and eggs for breakfast.' 'And what about us?' said the spoons. 'Without us nothing could be stirred.' 'And don't forget us; said the knives. 'Without us nothing could be cut in the kitchen.' 'And what about me?' said the stove. 'Without me there would be no use for any of you.' 'You are all wrong; said the wood in the woodbox. 'Without me there would be nothing for any of you to do.'"

There mother would pause dramatically. Then she would continue and say, "I slowly opened the kitchen door and there was silence: And now who do you think is the most important?" Teddy and Harold usually said it was the wood because we had to cut it. I maintained it was the axe, but I was always ruled out because the axe was not in the kitchen but on the wood heap. Ethel Edna always said the stove was most important. Dottie said it was the teapot only because she enjoyed a cup of tea. Then mother would conclude by saying, "No. Everybody was necessary because one could not do anything without the help of the other."

Yet another of mother's stories was, The Mouse who Fell in Love. "Yes," mother would say, "Monty Mouse was a real timid little bloke and he didn't really know how to approach Milly Mouse and declare his love for her. His trouble was that he didn't know how to express his feelings. He would pay her visits and give her bouquets of flowers and tasty bits of cheese. He would stutter in his attempts to talk to her. Now Milly Mouse was really in love with Monty Mouse and she longed for the day when Monty Mouse would tell her he loved her.

"One day Monty Mouse decided he would get some advice as to what he should do to declare his love for Milly Mouse. But who could he go to? He couldn't go to the wise old owl because the owl would gobble him up, and he certainly couldn't go to the cat. Then he thought, why not ask Danny the Dingo. Monty Mouse didn't know whether the dingo could help him or not, but he knew that Danny the Dingo was very cunning.

"So Monty Mouse went to visit Danny the Dingo and said, 'Mr Dingo, can you help me?' Danny the Dingo looked at Monty Mouse and replied, 'What sort of help do you want from me?' 'Well, you see,' said Monty Mouse, 'I'm in love and I don't know how to tell my lady love that I love her.' Danny Dingo yawned and replied, 'What you have to do is pull her tail.' 'What for?' asked Monty Mouse. 'What difference will that make?' 'Don't question me,' replied Danny Dingo, 'just go and do what I say, so now be off with you, I want to catch up on some sleep.'

"So Monty Mouse went to Milly Mouse and he pulled her tail. Milly Mouse became very angry and she squeaked and said, 'What did you do that for?' Monty Mouse replied with the sudden rush of words, 'Because I love you!' And Milly Mouse answered, 'And I love you too!'

"Then hand in hand," mother would conclude with a laugh, "they went and got married and they built a little house near the cheese factory and they had lots and lots of children, and they lived happily ever after."

Chapter 27

Many of the farmers in the South-west augmented their income by possum snaring. In some aspects to them it was better than trying to make a living out of dairying during the years of the Depression.

Several of the men employed by Millars used to snare possums in the possum season. Father was one of them. Possums are gentle night creatures who live on the tips of gum leaves. There would always be a parent tree with hollowed limbs where the possum lived and usually a patch of smaller gums growing nearby where they could feed. Us older boys, Tommy, Harold and I, would go out and set the snares and for every skin we brought home father used to pay us one shilling. He would then sell them for one pound a dozen.

There was an art in catching possums. First one had to find a reasonably straight limb fallen from a tree. Sometimes we would cut one down, then the limb was placed against the trunk of the tree or on a feeder tree at a seventy degree angle. The wire and twine snare would be tied around the limb. Then we would set the snare, which was a noose, so the possum climbing up or down the leaning limb would be caught around the neck, surely a terrible way to die. Trapping for possums was barred by law during their breeding season, but people continued to catch and hoard the skins until the possum snaring season opened.

It was in the late Twenties that the snaring of possums became illegal. By then it was almost too late because they were thinned out to such an extent that they almost became extinct. The rise in fox numbers and the spread of myxomatosis in the Fifties also added to their decline. If I caught a possum alive in the snares which I set I would let it go, much to the ire of my two older brothers and the amusement of father. A possum trapped in a snare only had to look at me and I would immediately let it go. That could be dangerous because they had sharp claws and teeth and endeavoured to bite me. But I usually overcame that by throwing a bag over them.

Possums made adorable pets. We always had a pet possum at one time or another. We had one called Joey who used to sleep in the ceiling and at dusk he would climb down from where he slept, then into the kitchen. When he had had his evening meal of apple or breadcrumbs he would usually go back into the ceiling. Sometimes he would come back into the kitchen when our household was asleep. Then he would climb upon mother's dresser and tip plates and cups and saucers groundward. One night he got into the cupboard and somehow prised the lid off a tin of golden syrup. Next morning there was syrup over everything. Mother was so angry she threatened to take him out in the bush and dump him, but father talked her out of that.

Another night Joey came into mother and father's bedroom and just as father awoke Joey scuttled out of the door and into the ceiling with father's pipe. As he only had one pipe that meant father had to go without a smoke. It was his turn to threaten to get rid of Joey. The following evening Joey again came out of the ceiling for his evening meal and brought back father's pipe, clenched in his paws. Father enticed him down with a handful of sugar and the exchange was made. But Joey went the way of most of our bush pets. One day the call of the bush overcame him and he returned to his kind.

Of the variety of wild pets we had, magpies were to me the most interesting. They were intelligent and could be very cunning and made good watchdogs. One day mother was in the front yard and she heard our pet magpie in the back yard calling out in alarm. She went around the back to investigate and a dugite was slithering through the geraniums. Mother went and got father's shotgun and blew that snake to pieces.

Our magpies, like our pet possums, always returned to their own. Father refused to cut the wings of our pet magpies. He always said if they wanted to go, let them. The pattern of them leaving would always be the same. First several wild magpies would appear and call out, our pet magpie would answer and run towards them. Then the flock would take off with our pet still grounded. He would call out after them. After two or three visits our pet magpie would take to the air with them and he would leave - and leave us with the knowledge that he would be happier with his own kind.

We had several wild piglets that father caught but they never really rated as pets because as they grew big enough they became part of the family's food supply. Once we had two wild ducklings, but they too left us one evening and flew off to join the wild ducks. The only pets mother baulked at having were bobtail goannas. They made good pets, but as soon as we mentioned bobtails to mother she would say No. Reminded her too much of snakes I suppose. Mother, like most bush people, seemed to have a personal vendetta against snakes.

One of mother's favourite snake yarns was about the time when father was farming at Hill-o-Waters in Waroona. Mother, father, Aunty Maude and a friend were playing euchre. They were busily engrossed in their game of euchre on the verandah, with the tall lamp throwing its glow and attracting night insects. Father felt something tighten, a sort of contraction on his leg under the table. He confessed later that he thought it was his partner's foot urging him to make trumps. The pressure became so insistent that father looked down and there was a tiger snake curled around one of his legs. Tiger snakes are reputedly one of the world's most deadly reptiles. Father knew that and with a mighty yeU he kicked out, sending the table, the snake and everybody flying backwards. Mother and Aunty Maude screamed and in the resultant bedlam the snake got away. Nevertheless that was the end of the euchre game. For that night anyway.

Chapter 28

If there was one thing father distrusted it was the motorcar. Though we seldom saw one in Yarloop. When father did he would denounce them loudly. In his horse and buggy mind he could not understand how anybody who could travel along at the unheard of speed of 30 miles an hour, almost sitting on a tank full of benzine and an engine that belched smoke, could be in their right mind.

One day Mr Bert Miles, a friend of father, bought a secondhand four cylinder car and offered to take father for a trip out to the swamps on a duck shoot, some ten kilometres west of the town. Father reluctantly agreed. He allowed me and Freckles to accompany him. Freckles and I sat in the back while father sat in front with Mr Miles. We chugged along the gravel road which led to the swamp country. The road deteriorated into a track full of potholes. We bumped and slithered along the boggy track while Mr Miles pointed out all the features of a motor being better than a horse. Father clung grimly to his seat, his unlit pipe clenched between tightly clamped jaws. Mr Miles was a non-smoker.

A gate loomed up ahead of us, the boundary of Mr Enright's property. As the car slowed down prior to stopping I called out to father, "I'll open the gate." Father replied, "No I'll open it." Mr Miles pulled up and father got out to open the gate. As Mr Miles drove through father closed the gate and lit his pipe, shielding it away from the car. We sat waiting for father. Mr Miles called, "You okay Bill?"

Father answered, "Be with you in a minute." After a few minutes wait, Mr Miles must have woken up to what father was thinking because he said with a laugh, "You can smoke in the car, there's no harm in it." Father emptied his pipe carefully on the heel of his boot and answered, "I dunno, I'd sooner be safe than sorry." We continued on our bumping rattling way. At last the ground became firmer and our speed quickened. We pulled up some hundred metres from the first swamp, father and Mr Miles picked up the shotguns and, with me and Freckles following, walked around the swamp. All we saw was a flock of ibis and a solitary blue crane. We returned to the car late in the afternoon, duckless.

Climbing aboard the Chevvy, Mr Miles said, "We'll be home in half an hour." Father grudgingly admitted he was right. We came once again to the gate and I sprang out, opened it and the Chevvy crawled through. We came to the wet patches on the road and the car slipped and slithered its way along the track. Mr Miles changed gears to overcome the heavy going while Freckles and I watched, fascinated by his hand and foot movements. It was then that we came to a particularly boggy patch and the front, then the rear wheels sank in the mud. The engine revved in protest. The car inched its way forward, then with the mud spinning from the back wheels we realized we were bogged. "Righto," said Mr Miles, "looks like we'll need a push."

Freckles, father and I climbed out of the car and pushed. The car inched imperceptibly forward, then the back wheels began to spin again. Mr Miles climbed from the Chevvy and directed us in collecting dry bulrush and pieces of bracken and we placed them under· the back wheels. He climbed back in the vehicle and with the engine roaring we endeavoured to push the car out of what was now a churned up quagmire. Father could contain his disgust no longer. "If this would have been a horse and cart," he said, "this wouldn't have happened." "I guess you're right Bill," said Mr Miles, with more cheer than he felt. "Now if you three wait here I'll walk to Enright's and try and get some help."

Enright's house lay half a kilometre up the fence we had come through earlier. Mr Miles walked off into the now gathering dusk, then the mosquitos arrived to plague us. As we were in swamp country it was a veritable breeding ground for massies and they attacked us in hordes. Father cursed the mosquitos and the motorcar. I suggested we make a smudge fire to ward off the massies but at the mention of fire father flatly refused, as in his imagination he could see the car exploding. So we sat in the back of the car and slapped while father slapped and cursed aloud.

An hour later we heard the sound of voices and the jingling of chains. Then Mr Miles and Mr Enright loomed up out of the dark leading a horse. The chains were quickly and efficiently attached to the front axle of the car and with Mr Enright leading the horse, and with a squelching of mud, the car was pulled effortlessly out of the bog. Mr Enright, turning to father, said with a grin, "The old horse is reliable, eh Bill?" Father replied, "At least you can depend upon them." Thanking Mr Enright for his help we climbed aboard the mud spattered Chevvy and continued on our way home, where we arrived covered in mud, a mass of mosquito bites and no ducks. In some ways I think father was satisfied with the result because it proved his point, that the horse was more reliable than the motorcar.

Chapter 29

It was 1932 and I was fourteen years of age. Mother and father reasoned it was better if I left school. Harold had left school the previous year. Tommy, who was now twenty years old, was employed by a Mr Cross, a travelling dentist. Mr Cross used to travel all over the State and Tommy would be away from home for about four months at a time. He was lucky inasmuch as he had regular employment, as it was almost impossible to get part-lime work, let alone a permanent job.

Mr A.O. Neville, Chief Protector of Aborigines, wrote to father and offered to teach Harold and I farming skills if we went to Moore River Native Settlement. It seemed that the Aborigines Department had a policy of finding jobs for, or appearing to teach farming skills to, educated Aboriginal youth. I always had an adventurous spirit and the prospect of going to Moore River sounded glamorous and exciting and I was eager to go. My brother Harold was just as excited as I was. Father was reluctant to let us go, but because employment was practically nil in Yarloop, he decided to let us.

Mother scrimped and saved to buy suitable clothing. One of the things she bought for us was a new pair of shoes each. There we were, two Aboriginal boys wearing shoes for the first time in our lives and leaving home for the first time also. After tearful goodbyes on mother's part and almost on mine, and a gruff goodbye and a quick handshake from father, we excitedly, and with some trepidation, boarded the Bunbury to Perth passenger train on the way to Mogumber and the Moore River Native Settlement. Immediately the train started on its journey I took off my shoes and socks. Harold did likewise.

We arrived in Perth on a Saturday at three o'clock in the afternoon. A man was waiting for us and, tersely bundling us into a car, he drove us to Bennett House, a hostel for travelling Aboriginals in Bennett Street, East Perth. And it was there we met Aboriginal people for the first time outside our own family. We were shown our room on the verandah by three giggling Aboriginal girls. At the evening meal we sat with the Aboriginal staff in the kitchen while the matron, who ran the hostel along with her husband, ate in the dining room. That was the first faint stirrings I had of discrim-ination.

To my brother and I Perth was a huge place and as there was no train to Mogumber until Monday we had all day Sunday to ourselves. One of the girls suggested we go to the pictures. So the five of us walked into Perth to see the movies and as it was a Sunday evening admission to the pictures was a silver coin. That is, you could see the film, which was usually an hour long, for threepence. We arrived back at Bennett House tired from the walk into town and we thankfully went to bed.

Sometime during the early hours of the morning I awoke to hear a rooster crowing and I suddenly became homesick. Not wanting to awaken my brother, I pulled the blankets over my head and sniffled dismally. Monday morning came and, packing our things, we began our adventure again, saying goodbye to the girls at the hostel. The matron's husband took us to the Perth railway station where we boarded the twelve o'clock mixed goods for Mogumber. When we were safely ensconsed in our carriage the matron's husband said a brief goodbye and left us. The engine gave a quick blast of the whistle and we were on our way to places in between and Moore River Native Settlement via Mogumber.

The country we travelled was of interest to us. It was so different from the jarrah and redgum forests of the South-west. Now, the country was of white gums interspersed with bulloak and sand plain. We arrived at Mogumber at three o'clock in the afternoon. As the train came to a halt we were met by a giant of an Aboriginal man. He was over six feet five inches in height, well built and had a mouthful of white shining teeth which flashed in his black face. Introducing himself as Jimmy Landy he picked up our suitcase and led us to a battered Dodge truck. He informed us that Mr Neal the Superintendent of the Mission was in the hotel and we had to wait for him.

An hour later Mr Neal appeared. He was of average height with a strong military bearing and sported a Kaiser Wilhelm moustache waxed at both ends. He grunted a brief gooday to Harold and I, and we climbed on the back of the truck. With Mr Neal driving we began the twelve-kilometre journey to the settlement. As we drew nearer to our destination we travelled through a young pine plantation, the first sign we had of the settlement itself. We drove over a run-through and then we were in the settlement.

The truck pulled up at a storehouse and a group of Aboriginal men began unloading stores. As we climbed down from the truck we were ringed by a crowd of Aboriginal boys and girls. Mr Neal told a fourteen-year-old boy to show Harold and I where the dormitory was and we walked with him to a long low building, the dormitory, which consisted of 24 iron beds stacked along the side of each wall. Georgie Anderson our guide pointed out two iron beds and said, "These two aren't being used, you had better have them." We placed our suitcase underneath the bed, watched now by a crowd of curious boys. We walked outside and stood on the verandah, the crowd milling around us. I was somewhat bemused by the scene. I had never seen so many Aboriginal people before in my life. I was to learn later that the population of the settlement was 450 people, consisting of Aborigines from all over the State.

The compound included a dormitory for boys and one for girls. There was the superintendent's house, storerooms, a dining room combined with a cook house and bakery, a hospital, a church, which also doubled as an entertainment centre, and a school. There were a few other buildings of an indeterminate nature, and a jail which had the soubriquet of The Boob. The whole area was ringed with a three-metre netting fence topped with barbed wire. That was called the compound.

To the west lay all the camps which were on the perimeter of the sports ground. Families tended to collect in groups. The largest group, the Wallams, comprised six brothers, all married, who had a large number of children each. People from the north of the State tended to camp together and they were generally elderly people who lived in hopes of returning one day to their own tribal areas.

They were all doomed to spend the remainder of their lives in the settlement. Looking back on Moore River, I would say it suffered from bad administration and lack of funds. It cost six shillings a day to keep a prisoner in Fremantle jail and two-and-six to keep an Aboriginal in Moore River. The dormitory crawled with bugs and fleas, while the dining room and cook house were crawling with cockroaches.

At night fights would break out in the girls' dormitory and sometimes in the boys'. Fighting down at the camps occurred often. Mr Neal never interfered in the quarrelling which took place outside of the compound, but he was quick to retaliate at any fighting or misdemeanour which occurred in the compound.

On this occasion, Mr Hedges, the second boss, as he was called, ordered several of the older boys to carry bread from the bakery to the dining room. Bert Kelly, a thin fifteen-year-old boy, was caught trying to steal a loaf of bread, and when the matter was reported to Mr Neal, he called all the compound boys into the dormitory and ordered Bert to drop his pants. Then with the trackers holding Bert, Mr Neal belted him with a cat-o-nine-tails unmercifully.

One day two sixteen-year-old girls who tried to abscond from the settlement were caught, brought back and locked in the boob. Next day they were taken down to the storeroom where they were both laid.over sacks of flour and Mr Neal flogged them with the cat until they wet themselves. He then ordered them to eat the flour. No attempt was actually made to teach me and my brother farming. One day Harold asked MrNeal why.

Mr Neal's cryptic reply was, "You're learning about all you'll ever learn about farming here." So as one was not supposed to question the Superintendent, we came to the conclusion that stabbing Zamia palms and picking roots in a paddock was to be the sum total of our knowledge of farming at the Moore River Native Settlement. After about three months we began to dislike Moore River and what it stood for. It was at that time we asked Mr Neal if we could leave the compound and move down to the camps. There was more freedom in the camps. One had to be punctual for meals in the dormitory. Breakfast was at seven o'clock, lunch at twelve thirty and supper at six. Everybody had to be in the dormitories at seven p.m., then they would be locked in for the night and the doors would not be opened until six thirty the following morning.

At the camp an old lady had offered to look after us. She was Lucy Movell and we called her Aunty Lucy. She lived alone with her grandson Joey, a spoilt brat fourteen years of age on whom she doted. Aunty Lucy allowed him to boss and order her around like a servant. Harold and I were the real servants of the camp. We had to cart wood and water for Aunty Lucy daily, while Joe lorded it over us all by doing nothing. Food was scarce in the settlement, no meat was supplied. One had to forage for bush meat if one wanted meat. The food in the compound was regular but not much better. There we had bread and fat, treacle for breakfast, a watery stew for the midday meal and bread and golden syrup for supper.

The fleas in Moore River were in plague proportions. The only way to get any sleep was to let them feed until they would stop biting, then you could throw back the bed clothes and kill them at leisure, only because they were too bloated to jump. Each morning the able-bodied men from the camps would get their work orders for the day. This was usually palm stabbing or root picking. I used to like palm stabbing the best. This meant stabbing a crowbar down into the centre of the Zamia palm and working it in a circular motion and loosening the palm fronds. The reasons why we had to kill the Zamia palms was because the nuts from them when ripe were poisonous to stock. Quite often we would come across a rabbit burrow and spend hours digging for the rabbits. We would then light a fire and cook the rabbit on the coals.

I was only in the settlement about two months when I had my first fight. I was fifteen years old and my opponent Henry was eighteen. This day he was rolling the remains of his tobacco into a cigarette, a precious commodity in Moore River, and when I accidentally bumped him he spilt the tobacco. He leaned forward and punched me in the back. Bewildered, I asked him why he had hit me and he snarled, "Because you spilt my tobacco." "Well," I replied, "I'm not scared of you." I immediately regretted my hot-headed reply, because he said, "Come on then, let's settle it."

There were several men in the camp and the prospect of a fight broke the monotony of the working day. Clarrie Spratt, an older brother of my mate, Jacky, a boy my age, jumped to his feet and said, "Okay I'll be referee." I hesitated, but I knew I had to fight or be branded as a coward, and I had said that I wasn't scared of him. I climbed reluctantly to my feet and Clarrie almost tore my shirt off me. I must have looked woefully thin beside the well built Henry, who stood flexing his muscles. I wished fervently that my brother Harold was present, but he had been sent on another job this day and was not with my gang. I remembered what father had taught us, take a punch and give two in return. But no way could I take a punch off this well muscled moron, who stood crouched waiting for me. I knew I had to be quick. So with everybody grouped around us, we circled one another warily and my opponent threw the first punch with blinding speed straight for my head. I barely jerked my head sideways in time as his fist grazed my temple.

We shaped up again and he threw a similar punch. I felt a tinge of anticipation. If he kept throwing punches at the same angle I knew I could match him. We squared up again and he threw his third punch. As he let go I threw my head sideways and stepped in towards him. At the same time I brought my left fist up in a looping uppercut and connected with his mouth. He staggered sideways and fell to his hands and knees.

Clarrie jumped in between us and said to Henry, "You had enough?" He jerked away, shook his head and pushing Clarrie aside he rushed at me. He threw his fourth overarm punch at my head, but this time I lifted my arms above my head and blocked the punch and poor Henry jumped back holding his now dislocated wrist. Clarrie insisted we shake hands and make friends but my opponent, because his pride was so badly dented, refused to shake hands with me. We gradually became friends over the weeks ahead. The settlement people could be mean and vicious and at other times they could be warm and kind-hearted.

Chapter 30

Monday was ration day for the people who lived in the camps. Every Monday morning people would trickle in to the compound store for the weekly ration of tea, sugar, flour, fat and tobacco and a couple of potatoes and an onion. Tobacco was the most prized possession in the settlement and acted as currency. The tobacco ration consisted of a stick of tobacco which was called a 'jockey'. A jockey was about two inches long by half an inch wide and was very strong. Though I had not yet taken on smoking, because I was working I was issued with a tobacco ration, along with my brother Harold. Tobacco was the currency used for gambling and during a game of two-up there was always someone willing to risk their ration in an attempt to win more. On this day my friend, Jacky Spratt and I wandered down to the two-up school. I usually gave my tobacco to Aunty Lucy but this day I decided to risk my jockey in the two-up game. I stood on the perimeter of the players. The ground was littered with sticks of tobacco. Felix Jackamurra was spinning and after he had headed the pennies I threw my jockey in the centre to set him. He spun again and tailed them. I felt exulted, I had doubled my stake.

I stood with the two jockeys held in my hand. Then it came my turn to spin, I threw the two jockeys into the centre and began my first two-up game. I spun the pennies and headed them, my friend Jacky urged me to pick up my stake, but for some reason I bet the lot. When my bet was covered I spun and headed them again. Now my stake consisted of eight sticks of tobacco. I left my stake and when I was set and spun again I headed them again. Now I had sixteen sticks of tobacco. In settlement terms I was rich. I decided on one more spin.

When the sixteen jockeys were covered I spun again. Once again I headed them. At the urging of Jacky I picked twenty two jockeys up and left ten on the ground to be set. But only three were covered, Jacky picked up the remaining seven. I then spun for the three jockeys and tailed them.

It seemed I had the major share of the tobacco amongst the players and I told Jacky he could keep the ones he had picked up. Arriving home I gave the lot to Aunty Lucy. For a few days she did a roaring trade with the tobacco. Keeping a few sticks for herself, she traded the remainder for tea and sugar, potatoes and onions and anything which was available. Though Joey got the lion's share of the food.

Death was always a time of mourning in the settlement. Sometimes we didn't know what family the death was in until we heard wailing from some particular quarter. Then at the sound of crying we would figure out who had died. Because of tribal difference many of the older people without relations lived on their own. Jack Henry was an old man from the Kimberley and he lived in a small kerosene tin humpy on his own. Two or three days had elapsed before those in the vicinity of his camp realized they hadn't seen him hobbling around it. Upon investigation he was found dead in his humpy, where he had lain for at least three days. His body was in a state of putrefaction.

It was evening when Jack's body was discovered and upon being notified, Mr Hedges, the second boss, came down to the camp to supervise the removal of the remains. The men who volunteered to remove the body wrapped him up in a blanket and with a stretcher between them, and myself in the lead (I had volunteered to carry the hurricane lamp), the carriers made a ghoulish-smelling procession to the cemetery, some quarter of a kilometre away from the camp.

Mr Hedges proved to have the weakest stomach of us all. As the men began to dig a grave to deposit the body in, he became violently sick. When the hole was dug deep enough (I hesitate to call it a grave) the body was lowered into the ground by hanging on to the corners at the ends of the blanket which was that poor soul's shroud.

It seemed to me that people in the settlement had a fatalistic attitude towards death. Nobody seemed to question why and when people died, though there would be lots of wailing. Somehow, I thought, there was too ready an acceptance of dying. Perhaps it was because everybody was isolated from the influences of the outside world. The rigours of the rules under which they lived, and which were tantamount to law, had hardened them against momentous occasions such as death. That night in bed I couldn't help thinking of old Jack Henry. What had he done to deserve such a lonely dying? And so far away from his own tribal country. Nothing. The only thing against him was that he was old and black.

Old Fred and Gummoo were another old couple who lived on their own. She was blind and Fred himself was fifty percent blind. Sometimes I would cart wood and water for them and they would unknowingly reward me with stories of their tribal country in the Kimberley. Sometimes they would sing, and to hear their two voices mingle and sing songs of their country in their own language was to me pure magic. Sometimes when Gummoo would be resting, Fred and I, the old and the young, would just sit staring into the fire. Sometimes my heart used to ache for him, though I didn't really know enough about my own feelings to know why. But I knew he was thinking of his own country and the years gone by. He knew that he would never see his tribal land again.

Chapter 31

Moore River Native Settlement was full of waifs and strays, mostly part Aboriginal children forcibly removed from their tribal parents. I remember one boy Teddy Parks. He was found in a wooden box in a park in Perth clutching a teddy bear. Hence his name. When these children were dumped in the settlement, if their name was too hard for white people to pronounce it would be anglicised or they would be given another name, thus losing their identity. Then there were the twin children of Asian Aboriginal parentage who were given the names of Orange and Lemon.

Many girls were sent out from Moore River Settlement to work for whites, some to city and some to rural areas. Theirs was a precarious existence. Bound by law to their white masters and mistresses, they were prey to all kinds of viciousness, none being less than that of sexual abuse. If a girl returned to the settlement pregnant, upon the birth of the baby, the mother after a lapse in time would be sent out to work again. Usually to a different area of the State. The baby would then become the property of the settlement.

Sometimes the fathers of these children would be sons of well to do families and property owners, and many a story has been told in the oral history of Moore River of babies being born, then done away with at birth and being buried in the pine plantation at the settlement by the native trackers or black police as they were sometimes called.

The native trackers were pathetic figures, usually old men in their fifties or over. They were chosen according to what part of the State they carne from. There was Billy Kimberley and Bluey also from the Kimberley district, Frank Narrier from the Midlands and Arthur Morrison from the south of the State. In reality they only had a nuisance value to adults but they were cruel and punished the children horribly for any misdemeanour, such as wagging school or not attending Sunday School. Their biggest value to the superintendent, Mr Neal, was that they carried out his orders without question.

One area of activity which the trackers seemed to enjoy was attempting to break up any love trysts between the young people. Clandestine love affairs flourished within the settlement, for where there is a will there is a way and relationships continued despite the zeal of the native police.

If a couple absconded from the settlement and were caught, as they usually were because city and country police stations would be notified, the man would draw an automatic sentence of six months while the woman would be returned under escort to the settlement. The men, if they insisted on absconding, would be banned from the settlement, but this did not deter them. Many of them had family in Moore River and they would sneak in under the cover of darkness to obtain scraps of food. These men were designated as outlaws and they enjoyed a certain amount of prestige amongst the inmates of Moore River because they defied authority.

Two such outlaws were the Dinah brothers Henry and Albert. They were full blood, handsome men about 25 and 27 years of age and both were known for their fighting prowess. The native police when hunting for them always travelled in threes and fours. Sometimes they would be hunted for on horseback, but the Dinah brothers always eluded their pursuers.

One night the farm machinery shed was set alight, the Dinahs were blamed for it and the hunt was trebled for their capture. Mr Neal himself rode out armed with a revolver to catch them, but they eluded their would be captors. I think the Dinah brothers took responsibility for setting alight to the shed because it gave them more prestige in their standing as outlaws in the eyes of the Aboriginal community at Moore River, by showing they were standing up against white authority. It was not until a few days later that two of the camp children admitted to starting the fire. Luckily no real damage was done as the thatched straw which the shed was made out of was wet from winter rains and didn't burn properly.

It was on a Monday morning as we reported for work that Bluey, one of the trackers, told my brother Harold and I that Mr Neal wanted to see us both. With some trepidation we confronted the superintendent in his office. We stood before his desk, while he kept on writing. He glanced up at us, sat back in his chair and said, "I have had a ring from the Aboriginal Department in Perth telling me to send you two home." My brother Harold said, "When do we go?" "On tomorrow morning's train," he told us. We walked out the door elated.

Word spread quickly that we were leaving Moore River and the sunny side of the nature of Nyungars came to the fore. My friend Jacky Spratt said wistfully, "I wish I could go with you." We spent the rest of that day packing our pitiful remaining gear into our battered suitcase. We had spent nine months in the settlement and we had made lots of friends. In some respects it was hard to leave but we were going home after a nine months absence. An added incentive was that Tommy was home and we hadn't seen him for nearly a year. Also we had a new baby sister whom we hadn't seen.

Next morning we were packed and waiting at the old Dodge truck. The faces surrounding us were now all familiar. There were cries of, "Don't forget to come back." My friend Jacky gave my hand a squeeze and we said an awkward goodbye. As the superintendent climbed into the driving seat we climbed on the back and were on our way to the siding with cries of, "Don't forget to write," and "Send me some tobacco," ringing in our ears.

We went through the pine plantation run-through and the Moore River Native Settlement was out of sight. Familiar ground clipped by us. Ground we had hunted on, stabbed palms on and picked roots on slipped by and at last we were in at the Mogumber siding. As we crossed the railway line we heard the approaching whistle of the train. The truck pulled up opposite the ticket office and Mr Neal purchased our tickets, which he gave to us. He also gave us two shillings to buy something to eat on the way. He shook hands with us and wished us good luck and the last we saw of him was his back as he entered the hotel.

A lot has been said and written about Moore River and its administrators, especially Mr Neal. But in all fairness it was a tough job and one had to be tough to handle it. There were a nucleus of Aboriginal troublemakers at the settlement and weaker men than Superintendent Neal had succumbed under pressure and left the job. Though I could never look upon Mr Neal as being a good bloke. As far as I was concerned he was too liberal with that cat-o-nine-tails.

Chapter 32

The mixed goods steamed its way down through the Midlands and at last we were approaching Midland Junction. A half an hour later we were on our way to Perth. We pulled in at the central railway station at three o'clock in the afternoon. Amid the hustle and bustle of the station we found out which platform the Perth to Bunbury passenger train started from. With five minutes to spare we sank thankfully back in our carriage on the last leg of our journey. As the train sped on its way it seemed to me as if the clicketty clack of the wheels over the rails was saying home, home, home, and my brother Harold and I were starting to become excited again at the prospect of seeing our family.

The passenger train sped past tiny places. Then we were in Waroona. We looked across the railway line at the house we used to live in and there were children playing out on the front verandah. I felt a lump in my throat at the scene, though not really understanding the depth of my emotions. I looked at my brother Harold and he had also a look of sadness on his face. Then the train sped on its way again with the next stop being Yarloop.

At last we were there. It was January, summer, when we had left home and now it was September, coming summer, when we returned. Tommy and Teddy were at the railway station to meet us. When Tommy saw me he said, "Crikey look at Jack." I was a gangling six-foot fifteen year old, while my brother Harold was almost as tall as I was. Teddy was all questions and Tommy, who had the predilection to stutter when excited, spat all over us. We walked up the railway line to the top yard, passing familiar things like the local hospital and the timber mill itself and its huge mound of sawdust.

Then there was the house. The tall lamp's glow could be seen shining through the window and the four of us quickened our pace. Father was the first to see us, as he was pegging a roo skin out on the jarrah tree. He shouted hello, dropped what he was doing and came quickly to us, grasping our hands. Then mother's arms were around my brother Harold and I and the children crowded around us. They had all grown as we had. Then May brought the new baby Judith out and she came to us immediately. There was too much of a resemblance between us all for baby Judith to regard us as strangers.

That evening we talked long into the night, father's concern being now that he had three strapping sons who had no prospects of employment. We had no immediate concern regarding unemployment. Father was still the bread winner. The months we had spent in Moore River, as far as work was concerned, were practically wasted. We went there with no working skills and left there with none, apart from root picking and palm stabbing. But we consoled ourselves with the fact that like us there were hundreds of men out of work and we were only a small part of the army of unemployed.

As we sat around the kitchen father knocked the ash from his pipe and said, "Well at least there's one thing you always can do, and that is do the hunting." And so we did. As soon as meat became scarce on our table Tommy, Harold and I would go hunting (Teddy was still at school). We were all good shots and knew how to handle guns efficiently.

Chapter 33

It was 1932 and the Depression hit the timber industry and consequently Yarloop. Millars began rostering work by allocating one week's work for single men and two weeks off, with two weeks on for married men and one week off. During father's week off, because of his hunting skills, he was able to augment the family larder more readily. We always acted as scouts in hunting for suitable honey trees. That is, those that were not too large to cut down, and when we found one we would carefully mark its location and at the appropriate time would show father where it was.

Tommy was twenty, Harold seventeen and I was a gawky fifteen year old. We all had the ability to swing an axe and consequently it did not take long to fell a honey tree. I consoled myself with the legitimacy of cutting a redgum down for honey, in that we were hunting for food.

Robbing a bee hive is an art. Father had the ability to judge which way the tree would fall and where the bulk of the tree containing the hive would be when the tree crashed to the ground. He scorned the simple bee smokers. Us boys would have a mixture of dry and green bush held in readiness. As the tree fell father would lead the way with his fire, rush to the tree and blow smoke into the entrance to the hive. We would then hand our fires to him and a smudge fire would be kindled with green leaves to create thick smoke. This does not kill the bees but dopes them for a few hours. Then the limb of the tree could be chopped open and the honey removed with comparative ease.

It was a Monday morning and the beginning of one of father's weeks off work. So he decided to go hunting in the hills for roo. Tommy had twisted his ankle playing cricket the day before and I wanted to go to the local swimming hole. So Harold and Teddy accompanied father. I arrived home just before sunset as hungry as any normal healthy fifteen year old could be. My hopes of an early supper were dashed when mother informed me we would all have to wait until the hunters returned. It was now near dark.

Tommy and I sat talking on the verandah, the younger children were requesting supper. Mother eventually conceded to their hungry queries by dishing out their food. It was at this point that Teddy burst through the door. He glanced fearfully around the room and said, "Is Father home?" Tommy replied, "No, why?" Mother came out of the kitchen and said, "Where have you been? It's getting late." Then Teddy told us what had happened and fear welled up within us.

As it was growing dark father had decided to take a short cut through a partly cleared, ringbarked paddock. We knew of the jersey bull and the cattle there and we always gave them a wide berth. Father and the two boys got halfway through the paddock when the cattle led by the bull milled around them. Father picked up a handful of sticks and kept them at bay and told the two boys to run for the fence a hundred metres away. An irrigation ditch ran through the paddock. The two boys scrambled over the ditch and through the fence. By this time it was almost dark.

They waited expectantly, then with growing anxiety, for father to loom up in the darkness. They called out, but no answering call came in reply. They waited with trepidation. It was then that Harold told Teddy to run home, thinking that father had gone home in a more circuitous direction.

Upon hearing what had happened Tommy sent me to get assistance from Bill Tower, our nearest neighbour. So with Teddy leading the way in the growing dark, Tommy, Mr Bill Tower and I walked rapidly up the railway line which ran past the ringbarked paddock where they had last seen father. Any minute we expected him to call out or loom up out of the darkness.

As we left the railway line we met Harold, who had been waiting for us. We climbed through the fence of the ringbarked paddock. We heard father's kangaroo dog Ruffy barking. We went to the dog, who was some hundred metres through the fence. Ruffy ran to us, then trotted off into the dark.

He led us right to where father was lying on the bank of an irrigation ditch. We grouped around him and tried to arouse him. Mr Tower took charge. He sent Tommy off to alert Mr Garlick, a near neighbour who owned a Chev truck. We waited for the truck to arrive.

A half an hour later the truck pulled up outside the fence. We had to carry father to the fence. Mr Tower undid the two top wires and we lifted father onto the truck. Mr Tower sent me and Teddy to tell mother to meet us at the hospital. We raced down the railway line and told mother what had happened. She quickly donned a coat, and leaving Teddy with the smaller children, mother and I walked rapidly down the railway line which ran past the hospital.

We saw the truck parked outside the hospital gate. A small group of people, including Tommy and Harold, stood near father. Mother ran to where he was lying on a stretcher on the verandah. The doctor walked quickly to mother and placed an arm around her shoulder and told her father was dead. Mother gave a short scream and slowly walked away. She walked over to us boys and said to me, "Go home and bring the children over to Mrs Tower's place."

As I ran up the railway line my mind was numb, I couldn't believe what had happened. Father was too vital, too full of life. I felt that what had occurred could not be. Upon reaching home I gathered the children and Teddy and I herded them over to Tower's house.

The day of the funeral came and people were in attendance from Harvey and Waroona as well as Yarloop, to pay their last respects to a man who was well known as a sportsman and a fellow worker. Tommy, Harold, mother and I stood with others around the graveside. My mind still refused to grasp the fact that father was dead. For some reason I felt angry, as if his death was unfair, and that it should not have happened to someone who was so full of the zest for living as he was. There again I thought, if I hadn't gone swimming on the day of his death and had gone hunting with them, it might not have occurred. Or, if Tommy had not twisted his ankle playing cricket and had gone with them the fatality could have somehow been prevented.

When we returned home after the funeral the house which father had practically built seemed doubly empty and bare, and emphasized the fact that he was no longer with us. Mother went into her bedroom and closed the door, and we her children, from the eldest to the youngest, left her to herself in her hour of sorrow, because we knew that's what she wanted. I will always remember the strength of mother through our bereavement. Though her face was swollen with grief, not once did she break down in front of any of us, her children.

It was not hard to reconstruct what had happened to father. As he had turned to leap the irrigation ditch, his foot had slipped and in falling, his head had struck the opposite bank, breaking his neck. He had died instantly. Our family stayed at Tower's place until after the funeral. Then we went home to our silent house, mother packed father's clothes and personal belongings away, leaving his one good coat hanging behind her bedroom door. I loved the smell of pipe tobacco which emanated from his coat. One day mother caught me with my face buried in it and to save more pain she packed his coat away with his other things.

In the cold light of reasoning, mother now found herself in a predicament. How could her family survive? Though she still had her Monday wash day at the local hospital, in desperation she got Tommy to write to the local Member of Parliament, who replied to mother's letter stating that we, as an Aboriginal family, were eligible for government native rations. That was a hard blow to mother's pride. After all those years of being independent and now at the death of father she had to accept native rations.

The rations consisted of tea, sugar, flour, soap and meat. Enough to supply our family of nine mouths. Ration day was every Tuesday. Mother wanted to get the rations from Mrs McPhee's store, but the Aboriginal Department had made the ration order out to Millars Co-op. The first ration day came and mother and I walked down town and went to the co-op. Mother's back was stiff with pride. Her lips compressed. For some reason it all seemed funny to me. I think it was mother's stance which evoked my mirth. As we walked out of the co-op laden with brown paper parcels I started to giggle. Mother paused in her angry walk and snapped at me, "What's so funny, what are you laughing at?" "I don't know mother," I replied, "I really don't know." Then suddenly we both exploded with laughter together.

Mother had three strapping sons in Tommy, Harold and I, but there was no employment and because of that our family unit started to lose its togetherness. So the three of us left home in search of work, only returning when we got a few days employment off some of the farmers. Mother hung on for six months after father's death. But the work day sound of the five o'clock mill whistle was a sad and constant reminder that father was not coming home. So after one last visit to the local cemetery to say a final goodbye to father and Kathleen, mother sold most of her possessions such as furniture. Some she gave away to friends. Then packing essentials in boxes and with her seven dependent children, she left Yarioop to go and live in Brookton on the Great Southern Railway, where she would at least have the comfort of being with her tribal sister Maude.

Chapter 34

Father's death meant my carefree days of boyhood were over. After mother's departure for Brookton, Tommy, Harold and I stayed on in Yarloop for a few months. Then one day I packed my few belongings and saying goodbye to my two older brothers, I jumped a goods train to Perth. I knew that I would have to find my own way in future. It was almost impossible to find employment, but I was tough and resilient.

I stood up in the railway truck and watched the little town of Yarloop recede into the distance. I knew my life as a boy was over and it was heart wrenching for me to leave it all behind. But I knew I would always carry the memories of my boyhood with me.

The war came and like countless other places in the world the lives of everyone were touched in Yarloop. Freckles went away to war and returned safely. Nick overcame his fear of heights and died when the bomber he was rear gunner in was shot down during an air raid over Germany. Harold was taken prisoner at Tobruk and was imprisoned in North Africa and then in Italy. He escaped and fought with the partisans. He saw the bodies of Mussolini and his mistress hung up by their heels in the streets of Milan and as he was a British subject, and an eye witness, he had to make a special report of the incident to the British war office in England. Gerry served in the Middle East only to die from a sniper's bullet at Wewak in New Guinea.

My roamings, by January 1937, found me in the Gascoyne, where I worked as a stockman throughout the war years. When I returned to the south of the State I found many changes in the structure of our family. Mother had married again. Tommy and Ethel Edna had married and had children. In 1970, after a lapse of 33 years, I was able to return to the school at Yarloop and present the school children with one of my books of poetry. It is here that my family and I leave you, and in presenting the triumphs and the tragedies of our lives, I hope it will inspire others to write of their lives as I have done.

Epilogue

It was pure coincidence which brought about that I was able to find mother's birthplace and her tribal relations. I had met Jack McPhee years before, when I was a boy at Moore River Native Settlement. But neither of us realized our relationship although he had the same name as mother.

When Sally Morgan was researching for the life story of Jack McPhee's book *Wanamurraganya,* the strands of mother's origins began to corne together. Jack and I met and talked over dinner at Sally's house in East Fremantle. Upon my talking with Jack and urged on by my questioning, he promised to make some enquiries when he returned to Marble Bar and Port Hedland. He was able to trace mother's family by the oral history network. He found out that mother's father was a Scotsman named Rory McPhee, one of two brothers who had children by two Aboriginal women, who were sisters. Jack was the son of one and mother was the daughter of the other.

Jack somehow managed to avoid the Government net which took part Aboriginal children away from their full blood mothers, probably because at the age of seven he became a stock boy. Mother had less chance of escaping because she was a girl. The memory of her being taken away has never left the minds of her tribal people, although she did not live long enough to see them again. Jack was even able to supply my Skin Name, which is Burungu. I am still trying to trace my father's Aboriginal family. The only information I have on his birth is that he was born in the district of Roebourne.

He had a sister called Mary who was placed in a mission and a brother Frank who was thrown from a horse into a stockyard rail and died from a broken neck. As father was to die years later. The cruel displacement of part Aboriginal children has caused many a heartache and still does today.